T0331060

Understanding the Technology Behind Online Offending

Understanding the Technology Behind Online Offending: A Guide for Professionals in the Criminal Justice System is a non-technical explanation of online offences by a cybersecurity expert, bridging the gap between the high-tech world of cybercrime and the non-technical professionals working within it.

The book begins by equipping the reader with a foundational understanding of how the Internet works before exploring the various ways that people can exploit the Internet to commit crimes. The reader is then introduced to some of the sophisticated ways that individuals may evade detection before we explore the organisations fighting to prevent and capture those offending online. The book includes a contributory chapter from solicitors at Stone King LLP to help the reader understand how the law is evolving to prosecute offenders. There is a further contributory chapter from psychologist Dr Ruth J Tully who discusses psychological risk assessment with those who offend online. The book concludes with important chapters looking at how professionals can keep themselves safe online and future directions of the Internet.

The book's intended audience includes all professionals who work with those who commit online offences, such as psychologists, solicitors, social workers, probation officers and police officers. The book is also suitable for those in training or graduate education.

Christopher Wise has been working within the IT industry for 20 years, for the last 8 years specifically within cybersecurity for organisations in the UK as well as abroad. He has provided consultancy services for the Independent Inquiry into Child Sexual Abuse (IICSA), Homeland Security (UK) and the Ministry of Defence. Christopher has given talks about online offending to professionals in criminal justice system at key conferences, including for the British Psychological Society Forensic Psychology Division. Christopher has a passion for security, privacy and helping non-technical professionals understand his area of expertise.

Jennifer Bamford is a Chartered and Registered Forensic Psychologist with 15 years' experience working in the criminal justice system in the UK. She has worked with many internet offenders from the point of investigation to post sentence risk assessments and has been involved as an expert witness in criminal and family law proceedings where online offending has been a central issue for the court. Dr Bamford has published previously on various topics in forensic psychology, with a specialism in sexual offending.

Understanding the Technology Behind Online Offending

A Guide for Professionals in the Criminal Justice System

Edited by
Christopher Wise and Jennifer Bamford

LONDON AND NEW YORK

Designed cover image: Getty Images @da-kuk

First published 2025
by Routledge
4 Park Square, Milton Park, Abingdon, Oxon OX14 4RN

and by Routledge
605 Third Avenue, New York, NY 10158

Routledge is an imprint of the Taylor & Francis Group, an informa business

British Library Cataloguing-in-Publication Data
A catalogue record for this book is available from the British Library

Library of Congress Cataloging-in-Publication Data
Names: Wise, Christopher, editor. | Bamford, Jennifer, editor.
Title: Understanding the technology behind online offending : a guide for professionals in the criminal justice system / edited by Christopher Wise and Jennifer Bamford.
Description: Abingdon, Oxon ; New York, NY : Routledge, 2025. | Includes bibliographical references and index.
Identifiers: LCCN 2024046404 (print) | LCCN 2024046405 (ebook) | ISBN 9781032896328 (hardback) | ISBN 9781032819679 (paperback) | ISBN 9781003543794 (ebook)
Subjects: LCSH: Computer crimes. | Digital forensic science. | Computer crimes—Investigation. | Computer crimes—Prevention.
Classification: LCC HV6773 .U53 2025 (print) | LCC HV6773 (ebook) | DDC 364.16/8—dc23/eng/20241209
LC record available at https://lccn.loc.gov/2024046404
LC ebook record available at https://lccn.loc.gov/2024046405

ISBN: 9781032896328 (hbk)
ISBN: 9781032819679 (pbk)
ISBN: 9781003543794 (ebk)

DOI: 10.4324/9781003543794

Typeset in Times New Roman
by codeMantra

Contents

Acknowledgements

We would like to extend our thanks to our contributors, Dr Ruth J Tully, Nick Wragg and Angus McWilliams, for giving up their time to contribute their expertise to Chapters 6 and 7. Thanks also to Nick Newman and Ian Richards for taking the time to critically review this book, and we are grateful to have received their respective endorsements. We would also like to thank the informal reviewers of this text, our colleagues, friends and family, who have given their time and offered valuable feedback.

Introduction

Jennifer Bamford

Why us?

In 2017 when working in independent practice, I began receiving a much higher volume of enquiries for psychological assessments for those involved with online sexual offending. These were predominantly men who had been arrested and who were under investigation for the possession of indecent images and/or communication offences. Whilst I had all the necessary training and experience in working with sexual offenders, I recognised that my understanding of the Internet and how it works was insufficient. Many of the men I interviewed had above average IT skills and the terminology they were using sometimes baffled me. It led to a self-directed crash course in many of the terms used and the fundamentals of how the Internet works, but it struck me as notable that throughout my various university degrees and clinical training I had not acquired sufficient understanding to work with internet offenders. I did not understand how these men could evade detection, sometimes for years. I did not know what file sharing sites were or how they worked. I did not know about the various terms used for different types of pornography (legal or otherwise), and I did not really recognise the massive scale of the developing problem; this has since been termed the 'pandemic of online offending'. I came to understand that because of this lack of knowledge, I felt ill-equipped to recognise and challenge, for example, when a client may have been minimising their behaviour, and this was problematic given the nature of my work as a forensic psychologist.

It was around this time that I met Chris Wise, who has written the vast majority of this book. As a cybersecurity expert Chris had the knowledge that I needed, but he was also adept at communicating it in a way that non-technical professionals could understand. Our collaboration with other psychologists and solicitors led us to become involved in delivering talks at professional conferences in which Chris would educate a range of professionals on how the Internet works, how people offend online, and how they might get caught. He would often be inundated with questions during and after each conference, and it became apparent that I was not alone in my lack of understanding. Solicitors, police, probation officers, therapists and other psychologists also struggled to understand this complicated topic. Chris was working full time on various projects at the time, including the Independent

Inquiry into Child Sexual Abuse (IICSA), and he no longer had the time to offer his expertise at conferences. But this did not stop the questions coming from myself and my colleagues, and hence the idea for this book was born.

Our contributors

Within Chapter 6, we have the invaluable input of solicitors Nicholas Wragg and Angus McWilliams from Stone King LLP who are both well-experienced solicitors working with those who have faced prosecution for online sexual offending. The Stone King team has been central over the years in drawing together the experiences of various professionals at conferences so that we might be able to share and learn from one another in this complex area. They have the important job of staying ahead of changes in the law, and their shared experiences in court have been synthesised within Chapter 6.

Nicholas Wragg is a specialist criminal justice Solicitor and Higher Rights Advocate. He handles cases at all levels throughout England and Wales, in the police station, Magistrates' Court, Crown Court and Court of Appeal.

Angus McWilliams is a specialist criminal justice Solicitor. He deals with cases across the criminal justice arena throughout England and Wales in frontline criminal practice.

In Chapter 7, Dr Ruth Tully discusses the available risk assessment tools used to assess those who have engaged in sexual, stalking or extremism offending which may have an online element. This chapter is especially useful for psychologists new to risk assessment but may also be useful for other professionals who need to read and interpret the psychological assessments of their clients, e.g. solicitors.

Dr Ruth J. Tully is a Consultant Forensic Psychologist in private practice in the UK. She is a Registered Practitioner Psychologist with the Health and Care Professions Council (HCPC) and is chartered by, and a Fellow of, the British Psychological Society (BPS). Dr Ruth Tully has vast clinical experience in various areas of assessment and intervention, with a particular interest in violent offending (including terrorism), sexual offending, learning disability, developmental disorders, neuropsychology and personality disorder. She has also published research articles and book chapters in these areas. Dr Tully regularly conducts expert and clinical assessments in criminal, prison and family law cases.

Cybercrime, online sexual offences and online harm

In approaching the task of writing a book about the broad topic of online offending, it became evident that we needed to make a distinction between what is termed "cybercrime", online sexual offences and other online harm. This distinction is made within Chapters 2 and 3, where we break down some of the offences that comprise each category. Broadly speaking, cybercrime is predominantly a national security issue, comprising offences such as phishing, whilst online harm and online sexual offences are a public safety issue. Throughout this book, we use the term "online offenders" to refer to individuals who commit any type of offence using the Internet, and we refer differently to those who commit online harm or online sexual offences. In Chapter 8, we discuss the collaboration between professionals and agencies working in these distinct areas of cybercrime, online sexual offending and online harm to try and tackle the broader problem of internet-facilitated crime. Whilst professionals working in these distinct areas employ the assistance of police, legal representatives and sometimes experts, we don't see, in practice, a widespread understanding of the Internet and how to effectively police it. The purpose of this book is to demystify those elements of the Internet in the hope that all professionals working on both sides of the problem will have a more informed understanding.

The scale of the problem

If you're reading this book, you are likely to be aware at least to some degree of the significant increase in online crime over time. As our lives become increasingly more 'digital', and we place more of our personal information online, so increases our vulnerability for potential exploitation. Online offending, in general, is becoming not just more prevalent but more sophisticated, and it affects all of our lives, professionally and personally. It is beyond the scope of this book to go into detail on every form of online offending. However, we have tried, within Chapters 2 and 3, to offer some understanding of the different ways that the Internet can be used for illicit behaviour, making the distinction between cybercrime and offences that cause online harm.

Prior to 2015, the crime rate for England and Wales demonstrated a steady reduction; between June 2014 and June 2015, the crime rate reportedly fell by 8%. However, this statistic did not include cybercrime and was, therefore, a false representation of crime as a whole. In October 2015, when cybercrime was considered within the official statistics, the crime rate almost doubled from 6.5 million offences to 11.6 million offences (Travis, 2015). However, cybercrime can be difficult to define and, therefore, measure; the Office for National Statistics acknowledge that 'cybercrime' is not a specific crime type that is collected, but rather the Crime Survey includes offences under the Computer Misuse Act as well as online fraud (Office for National Statistics, 2022). Whilst cybercrime can impact individuals and consumers, there is also significant targeting of businesses. By April 2024, 50% of businesses and 32% of charities reported having experienced some form of cybersecurity breach within the previous 12 months costing an average of £1,205 to the business. For medium and large businesses, who were targeted more frequently, the cost was an average of £10,830 (Home Office, 2024).

Whilst we comment in Chapters 2 and 3 on the various forms of offending that are committed digitally, a focus of this book (especially within Chapter 6 and the Concluding chapter) is on offences which cause sexual harm. Online sexual offences make up a high proportion of online crime and are, arguably, some of the most damaging offences that can be committed online. The WeProtect Global Alliance report from 2023 offers helpful insights into the growing nature of online sexual abuse. The report concluded an 87% increase in reported child sexual abuse material from 2019, whilst the National Society for the Prevention of Cruelty to

Children report an 82% rise in online grooming crimes against children within the last five years (NSPCC, 2023); children are increasingly being abused online, and the abusive images are becoming increasingly available. Of further concern is the use of generative artificial intelligence (AI) in producing child abuse material, which has been increasing consistently (Thiel et al., 2023). Indeed, the Internet Watch Foundation (2023) discovered an online manual that teaches offenders how to refine the prompts that they input into an AI tool to train it to create realistic images. As this book will go on to describe, the use of AI tools is no longer something confined to IT experts but is becoming an increasingly user-friendly and accessible form of technology to the masses.

Why what we do matters

Chapter 8 gives us the opportunity to talk about all the great work being done in detecting and redirecting online offenders. Through collaborating with professionals, such as StopSo and The Lucy Faithfull Foundation, it is evident that there are compassionate and curious professionals wanting to help rehabilitate those who have offended online. We will also highlight various global efforts in tackling online sexual offending and highlight some key examples of successful inter-agency working.

Professionals working in this field will know that those who offend online represent, sometimes, a unique group. Online sexual offenders only (no contact offending)[1] can often present with a very different set of risk factors to contact sexual offenders, and our developing experience with this client group is helping us all to make sure that rehabilitation efforts are successful.

Online sexual offending is sometimes mistakenly seen as a victimless crime, especially by the clients we work with. This can be a significant cognitive distortion and, within my own clinical experience, the most common (see Chapter 4 for a review of common cognitive distortions in online offenders). Additionally, the rise of 'paedophile hunters' is a complex and polarising issue. However, for victims the impact is real, and it is significant. For example, the Internet Watch Foundation (IWF, 2023) reported that the number of webpages hosting category A material had more than doubled between 2020 and 2023, and the IWF report that "the data shows some of the very worst sexual abuse the IWF finds is being perpetrated upon the youngest, most helpless children, with babies and toddlers being subjected to acts including rape and sexual torture".

Reoffending rates are difficult to accurately assess and vary between contact sexual offenders and non-contact sexual offenders; however, a reasonably robust finding is that those sexual offenders who commit both online and contact offences are more likely than online-only offenders to reoffend (e.g. Elliot et al., 2019). Nevertheless, as identified by a police officer during a conference we attended in 2019, *"we only catch the stupid ones"*. For reasons that will be made clear within this book, when managing those who offend online, more so than with many other offending groups, there may be a greater reliance on internal risk management (i.e. your clients' genuine motivation to desist and their insight into ways of managing their own risk), rather than external risk management strategies.

How to use this book

In writing a book about cybercrime and online harm, both Chris and I were conscious that we did not want to further equip online offenders with knowledge that would facilitate their behaviour. It is important to preface this text by saying that all of the information contained herein is available online; if someone wishes to commit an online offence and attempt to evade capture, the wider Internet is unfortunately a source of potential assistance. This book is clear in its aim; we want to help professionals working in this area to better understand online offending so that we can find, treat and/or manage online sexual offenders in a more informed way.

Those apprehending and managing people who offend (i.e. Police and Probation Officers): For those working in detection or risk management, we hope this book will give you some insights into the ways that online offenders may try to evade capture and how that relates to your management of them. We will try to be exhaustive in thinking about the creative and intelligent ways that online offenders try to hide their behaviour so that 'no stone is left unturned'. Chapters 5, 8 and 10 might be especially relevant for you.

Those representing or prosecuting defendants (i.e. Solicitors and Barristers): We hope that this book will further your understanding of the method(s) through which a defendant may have offended. This may have important ramifications in terms of identifying the most likely charge/sentence or challenging such. We would direct you to Chapters 1, 4 and 5 as a source of helpful information in this regard. Chapter 7 might assist in understanding how an expert might approach assessing risk for the defendant.

Those treating and assessing offenders (i.e. Psychologists and Therapists): If you are working in therapy with or clinical assessment of people who have offended online, our hope is that this book will give you the confidence to challenge and treat your clients effectively. We hope that by the end of this book you will have a better understanding of some of the important questions to consider in your clinical work, and we will offer some guidance in this respect during relevant chapters. Chapters 1, 4 and 6 might be especially helpful.

For all professionals, we would suggest reviewing Chapter 9 for some important tips on how to keep yourself safe as individuals and professionals.

Almost 30 years ago, Davis et al. (1995) posited that a key element in finding those who sexually offend online is *"adequate training and awareness by criminal justice agencies"* (p. 47) and that *"those officers and agencies with expertise in the area must be willing to share their knowledge with others"* (Durkin, 1997). We hope that this book will meet that aim and be informative to a range of different professionals.

If you would like to contact the authors, please feel free to do so at: enquiries@ cyberwise.courses

If you are interested in online training on the topics included in this book, and other related topics around the Internet and online offending, you can find more information at: cyberwise.courses

Note

1 It is important to highlight that the psychological harm caused through non-contact offending should not be viewed as any less significant than contact offending. It is beyond the scope of this book to explore the impact of different forms of offences on those who are victimised, although within our Concluding chapter we consider some of the widespread impact of online offending in more detail.

References

Davis, L., McShane, M., & Williams, F. P. (1995). Controlling computer access to pornography: special conditions for sex offenders. *Federal Probation, 59*(2), 43–48.

Durkin, K. F. (1997). Misuse of the internet by pedophiles: Implications for Law Enforcement and Probation Practice. *Federal Probation, 61*(3), 14–18.

Elliot, I. A., Mandeville-Norden, R., Rakestrow-Dickers, J., & Beech, A. R. (2019). Reoffending rates in a U.K. community sample of individuals with convictions for indecent images of children. *Law and Human Behavior, 43*(4), 369–382.

Home Office. (2024). Official statistics: cyber security breaches survey 2024. Retrieved September 13, 2024, from https://www.gov.uk/government/statistics/cyber-security-breaches-survey-2024/cyber-security-breaches-survey-2024

Internet Watch Foundation. (2023). *'Extreme' category A child sexual abuse found online doubles in two years*. Retrieved February 11, 2024, from https://www.iwf.org.uk/news-media/news/extreme-category-a-child-sexual-abuse-found-online-doubles-in-two-years/

Internet Watch Foundation. (2023). *Prime Minister must act on threat of AI as IWF 'sounds alarm' on first confirmed AI-generates images of child sexual abuse*. Retrieved February 11, 2024, from https://www.iwf.org.uk/news-media/news/prime-minister-must-act-on-threat-of-ai-as-iwf-sounds-alarm-on-first-confirmed-ai-generated-images-of-child-sexual-abuse/

NSPCC. (2023). *82% rise in online grooming crimes against children in the last 5 years*. Retrieved February 11, 2024, from https://www.nspcc.org.uk/about-us/news-opinion/2023/2023-08-14-82-rise-in-online-grooming-crimes-against-children-in-the-last-5-years/

Office for National Statistics. (2022). *Cyber crime in the UK 2018–2021*. Retrieved September 13, 2024, from https://www.ons.gov.uk/aboutus/transparencyandgovernance/freedomofinformationfoi/cybercrimeintheuk20182021

Thiel, D., Stroebel, M., & Portnoff, R. (2023). *Generative ML and CSAM: Implications and Mitigations*. Retrieved February 11, 2024, from https://stacks.stanford.edu/file/druid:jv206yg3793/20230624-sio-cg-csam-report.pdf

Travis, A. (2015). *Crime rate in England and Wales soars as cybercrime is included for first time*. Retrieved September, 13, 2024, from https://www.theguardian.com/uk-news/2015/oct/15/rate-in-england-and-wales-soars-as-cybercrime-included-for-first-time

WeProtect Alliance. (published 17th October 2023). *Global Threat Assessment* 2023. Retrieved February 11, 2024, from https://www.weprotect.org/global-threat-assessment-23/#full-report

1 The Internet simplified

Christopher Wise

Key terms for this chapter and beyond

In this chapter, we will explain some fundamental principles of how the Internet works which includes some technical terms. These are terms that we refer back to throughout the book in later chapters and so we have compiled the following brief glossary to help:

Encryption – The simplest description of encryption is that it protects any information or data by using complex mathematical algorithms to make the data unreadable to anyone without the "key". Keys take many forms depending on the type of encryption, but it is easiest to think of them as a password to unlock the data.

File path – It is the location of a file on any file system, such as a USB stick or hard drive.

HTTP (Hypertext Transfer Protocol) – It is the language used to send and receive web pages between devices.

Human-readable – Human-readable is a term used to describe any code or data that can be naturally read by a human, as opposed to machine-readable. Machine-readable is where data can only be understood by a computer.

Intranet – Intranets are private networks only accessible by a company or the employees of an organisation. They are generally only accessible using approved devices.

Indexing – This is the name given to the processes used by search engines to find and catalogue websites, in the same way that a librarian may catalogue all books in a library.

IP address – Internet Protocol address is the unique number given to any device connecting to a network either via WiFi, cables or a mobile phone network.

Man-in-the-middle (MITM) attacks – Within cybersecurity, different types of techniques used by hackers have various names. An MITM attack is where a hacker tricks a user into connecting to their malicious hardware or software and by doing so is able to intercept all traffic from

---

DOI: 10.4324/9781003543794-1

those devices. A typical example is setting up a fake WiFi network in a public space and tricking unsuspecting victims into connecting to it, usually presenting some form of counterfeit login or even payment page to steal sensitive data or credit card information (see Chapter 8 for more on this and how to minimise the risk of this attack).

Operating system – Any computer, mobile phone, smart TV or any other type of smart device is a combination of hardware and software. The operating system is the software 'brain' of a computer and handles all core functionality.

Peer-to-peer (P2P) networks – P2P networks are most commonly used to share files. With the right software, anyone can connect their computer to a P2P network and use it to download and share files. Unlike a traditional download, where your machine (the client) downloads a file from a remote server, all the peers on the network act as both clients and servers. The more peers who have the same file, the faster the download. As a result of the shared ownership of files, users have a perceived level of anonymity, being one of many with a potentially illegal file.

Router/modem – This is the device that most businesses and homes use to connect to the Internet and is generally provided by your internet service provider (ISP). It creates a network in your home and allows multiple devices to share that internet connection and to communicate.

Torrent – A torrent file contains metadata about a file or collection of files and is most often used to download a file from a P2P network. A torrent file doesn't mean you have the content; only the locations and file names needed to start the download.

Web page – It is a collection of text, images, videos and code that make up the content that we can view on our mobile devices or computers in a web browser.

History of the Internet

To understand how people misuse the Internet, we must first understand what the Internet is. The simplest explanation is that the Internet is a network of connected computers communicating, sometimes at nearly the speed of light, over vast distances, using giant cables beneath the oceans and via satellites thousands of miles above the earth's surface. Its origin is well documented and spans decades. Like other technologies discussed in later chapters, the US Department of Defence had a significant role, as did many major universities. Nevertheless, the World Wide Web as we know it today was born in 1990 and created by Tim Berners-Lee, a British scientist (Berners-Lee & Fischetti, 1999).

So, what was the first website? While Tim Berners-Lee was working at the European Council for Nuclear Research, known as CERN, he set out to solve the challenge of automated data sharing between scientists and universities worldwide. As a result, the first website belonged to CERN. It is still active today and can be viewed in a simulated version of an early web browser called the line-mode browser (https://info.cern.ch/). After this point, other academic institutes began creating websites, and the Internet began to grow. By the end of 1993, there were 130 websites (Couldry, 2012). In 1994, websites for the general public started to appear, with 2,278 websites making up the entirety of the Internet (Total Number of Websites, n.d.). Today, that number stands at over 1.5 billion (Total Number of Websites, n.d.).

At its creation in 1990, approximately 2.6 million people were using the Internet. By 1995, this had ballooned to 44.4 million people, and Yahoo, eBay and Amazon.com had been created. By 2023, it was estimated that 5.3 billion people would use the Internet regularly, equivalent to 65.4% of the world's population. By 2025, this figure is estimated to increase to 6.54 billion (Petrosyan, 2024).

Malevolent intent

My first internet experience was in 1994 when my school purchased its first computer with a modem. I was a founding member of the "Internet Club", where I and five other students met with our chemistry teacher to look at everything interesting on the Internet. There was only one computer, so we would take turns controlling the mouse and keyboard. A few years later, I stumbled across my first example of the Internet being used for malevolent intent in the form of the "Jolly Roger's Cookbook", as it was labelled at the time. The Jolly Roger's Cookbook is a series of text documents that originated from a book published in the 1970s called the "The Anarchist Cookbook", with each text document including instructions for bomb-making, drug manufacture, how to kill a person and telephone hacking (otherwise known as "phreaking"). This document was shared across the Internet during the 1990s and can still be found today. In the UK, possession of "The Anarchist Cookbook" without reasonable excuse has been successfully prosecuted (Barnes & Mackie, 2022). It has also been linked to several violent incidents, including the 2005 London bombings (Dokoupil et al., 2011).

Areas of the Internet

Put simply, the Internet is divided into three sections or types. This is easily visualised as an iceberg (see Figure 1.1). The most easily seen top portion is the Clear or Surface Web. This is the part of the Internet that we use every day, and it is easily found via search engines such as Google, Bing or Yahoo. It includes websites, blogs, news, social media and anything else you can easily find by searching, typing in a web address or clicking a link in an email.

The next layer of the iceberg is the Deep web. This is the largest part of the Internet and is represented by the vast part of an iceberg that sits beneath the water.

This not-so-easily-seen part is anything that cannot be found or *indexed*. Types of data considered to be in the deep web include:

- Private content – anything that requires a login to access, such as emails, subscription services, online banking or internal company websites, also known as intranets. This would also include cloud storage services such as iCloud, Google Drive and Microsoft OneDrive.
- Databases – less widely known or used. These vast data repositories include academic and library databases, legal documents and health records.
- Web archives – once something is published online, it is rarely forgotten. Vast archives exist online, keeping copies of old websites and articles. If you want to see how the first version of Google looked, you can find it at https://web.archive.org/.

The third and final part of the Internet is the Dark Web, arguably considered the most sinister side of the Internet and represented by the tiny point at the very bottom of our iceberg, given its comparatively small size. The dark web has developed a reputation for being the "seedy underbelly" of the Internet, a place where illicit activities take place and criminals operate undetected, from selling drugs on eBay-like marketplaces to human trafficking and hitmen for hire. Unfortunately, this

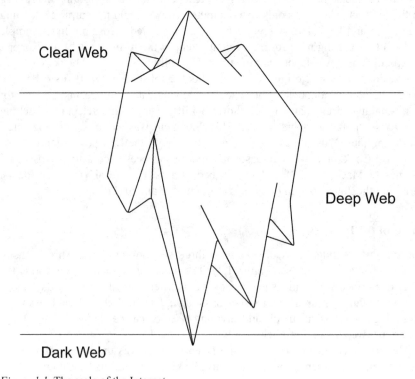

Clear Web

Deep Web

Dark Web

Figure 1.1 The scale of the Internet.

is all true. However, the dark web does have some legitimate uses. For example, it provides a secure platform for whistle-blowers, journalists and people living under oppressive regimes. We will delve much deeper into the dark web in Chapter 4.

As you can see from the above diagram, the different types or layers of the Internet are very different. Due to the nature of the deep and dark web, it is challenging to truly calculate the percentage split between them, and no reliable figures exist. However, it is generally accepted that the clear web makes up 4%–5% of the Internet, and the dark web only 0.01%, with the remaining 94% making up the deep web.

In percentage terms, the dark web is tiny but a tiny part of something huge. To put that 0.01% into perspective, the size of the Internet is measured in zettabytes (ZB), with one ZB equal to a trillion gigabytes (GB); the average smartphone has 128 GB of storage. In 2020, a study estimated that the Internet was 64 ZB (Taylor, 2023). Based on those figures, if the dark web were a movie, it would take roughly 730 million years to finish! The Internet is a truly massive place, and it is constantly growing.

How the Internet works

Now that we understand the internet's size, scale and categories, let's explore its workings a bit more. When speaking with non-technical people about the web and how it works, I like to use the post office analogy. We will use this analogy throughout this book to better understand how different technologies alter the journey and appearance of our internet use.

Before you can use the Internet, you need a device to access it. In our post office analogy, this could be considered the pen and paper required to write our letter. Today, we have many options: smartphones, TVs, gaming consoles, and, in some cases, fridge freezers. The number of Internet-connected devices in a modern home is staggering. One key point to consider throughout this book are the major components of these devices and the infrastructure supporting them, who creates and maintains them and where the responsibility for protecting us from harmful content could lie.

First, we have the device itself. In the case of Apple devices, Apple creates both hardware and operating systems and provides its own Safari web browser. When looking at other manufacturers, it becomes more complicated. Many other phone manufacturers use the Android operating system, which is free and open-source, although technically created and maintained by Google. On top of that operating system, we will have social media applications, web browsers and many other applications owned and operated by more companies. We also have to consider the networks we're connecting to and passing through and the networks used by those tech companies to run their software and make it available globally. When communicating with someone across the Internet, the same complex web exists.

When you visit a website, hundreds of requests are made behind the scenes, each asking for the pieces that make up the page or email you are looking at. These pieces are images, text, the code that makes clever animations happen when you click a menu, and the formatting that turns text into tables and columns. Imagine these requests as metaphorical letters sent from your computer or mobile phone to the computer or server with that website stored on it (the recipient of your letter). Much like the letter you are sending, certain pieces of information are needed to ensure it gets to where you intend (the recipient's address) and so that you will get the response you need (your address). You also need the infrastructure to take it from your home to its destination and ensure that any replies get back to you.

Key technologies to understand

Operating system. Every smart device has an operating system. This sophisticated piece of software starts with the device's hardware. It ensures that all the hardware works together and that applications can be installed and work smoothly together. Without an operating system, most devices would be unable to function. When you install an app on your smartphone, the operating system facilitates this and makes sure it works.

Applications or apps. A web browser is an application like your calendar, preferred messaging services or document editing software like Microsoft Word.

Protocols. For computers across the globe to communicate despite being built by different manufacturers and running different operating systems, there must be a common understanding between them. This shared understanding is where protocols come in, which you can consider to be like languages; they are defined by international standards and adhered to by all manufacturers. Describing the vast number of protocols is beyond the scope of this book, and even the most die hard IT specialists will be able to name only a small percentage of them. One important thing to note is that protocols generally work together; a low-level protocol will allow the hardware of two computers to communicate, and the higher-level protocols are used by the software, like your web browser. Using our post office analogy, the low-level protocol is the agreed-upon process for sending a letter; you buy stamps, put your letter in an envelope, and take it to the post office. The higher level would be the equivalent of ensuring you write the letter in a language the recipient understands. It wouldn't work well if you sent a letter to someone in a language they don't speak!

For our purposes, there are two key protocols to be aware of:

- Transmission Control Protocol/Internet Protocol (TCP/IP) – This is a lower-level suite of protocols. All computers connected to the Internet use this protocol and it is the source of IP addresses described below. The IP was originally created by Defense Advanced Research Projects Agency (DARPA), a US Department of Defense agency.
- HTTP – Next to TCP/IP, this is the foundation for what we know as the Internet. This protocol allows for the transmission of web pages. Most web pages are written using HTML. HTML is mostly human-readable, with small amounts of code that control formatting and layout.

IP address. A computer must have an address to be connected to any network, especially the Internet. Just like every building has an address, every computer has an IP address. A key point is that when accessing the Internet, all devices in the same home appear to be from the same IP address. It is only the router inside the home that knows which specific device is communicating with which websites, but this information is private and typically not stored. IP addresses are part of the TCP/IP suite of protocols used to connect devices on the Internet, as described above. Private networks also use IP addresses, including those in your home.

Domain Name System (DNS). The DNS is the address book of the Internet. As we've covered, every computer on the Internet has an IP address, but if you wanted to access Google, typing its IP address every time wouldn't be very meaningful or easy, especially considering IP addresses can change. Instead, we use domains like google.com, wikipedia.com, bbc.co.uk, etc.

URL (Uniform Resource Locator). A URL is simply the address to a unique resource on the Internet. It includes the domain and any information that comes after it. Much like a file on your computer has a file path, content on the Internet follows a similar pattern. Using this example from Wikipedia (https://en.wikipedia.org/wiki/File:Submarine_cables.png), we can break it down into the following pieces:

- **https://** – This tells your computer that the protocol to access this resource is Hypertext Transfer Protocol Secure (HTTPS).
- **en.wikipedia.org** – This is the domain, which is the human-readable address that is looked up on the DNS directory to find the IP address it points to.
- **/wiki//** – Much like folders on your desktop, this is the path to the image.
- **Submarine_cables** – It is the name of the file.
- **.png** – It is the type of file, in this case an image.

Transport Layer Security (TLS). It is also known as Secure Sockets Layer (SSL). In the early days of the Internet, all data was shared in what is commonly called "the clear" by IT professionals. This meant there was no encryption of any kind, and any computer that the data passed through or shared a network with could easily view the information about who and where that data was coming from, going to, and the content. Similar to sending a postcard, there is nothing to stop anyone handling that postcard from reading the message on the back. It wasn't until 1994 that one of the early web browsers introduced HTTPS (a secure version of HTTP). HTTP was still used but wrapped in a layer of encryption provided by SSL. This significantly increased the security of internet use, and online payments or banking wouldn't be possible without it. Using HTTPS is like taking a letter and putting it in an envelope that can only be opened by the person it's delivered to.

Web browser. The web browser is the software used to render content we can see and interact with from the Internet. The earliest browsers were relatively simple compared to their modern counterparts. We now have many more choices in which web browser we want to use beyond those that used to come bundled with the operating system of our PCs. One of the most significant changes to browsers is the increase in the privacy and security that they offer, and there are even browsers that have been explicitly designed to increase privacy online. We will talk more about those in detail in Chapter 4.

Putting it all together

Now that we understand some key concepts, let's combine them with our post office analogy. The router is essentially a high-speed post box; it is the device that allows you to send and receive data across the Internet at great speeds. When you connect a device to a router via WiFi or by plugging in a cable, the router gives it an IP address. These private IPs are not visible outside of your home network and change constantly; just disconnecting your laptop from WiFi and reconnecting it will generally mean you get a different IP address. You can almost view this as the name on a letter. It tells you who the intended recipient in your household is, but it doesn't mean much to your mail carrier.

Routers do not care about the higher-level protocols such as HTTP and only worry about TCP/IP connections to the Internet, in the same way that the post office isn't interested in the content of your letters, just at making sure they get from A to B. All devices using the same router appear to the outside world using the same public IP issued by the ISP (e.g. BT Broadband Internet). Whilst also being fairly dynamic, a router may use the same IP address for days, weeks or even months at a time. A change in IP address is usually caused by restarting the router or losing the connection to your ISP.

ISPs keep detailed records of the IP addresses used, by which customer, and when. The retention of this data varies depending on regulations for a given country but can range from months to years. Within the UK, the Investigatory Powers Act was introduced in 2016. Part of this new legislation included creating Internet Connection Records (ICRs), which meant that with senior judge approval, Internet providers and phone companies could be ordered to store people's browsing history for up to 12 months. This resulted in significant backlash from privacy groups and advocates (Liberty, n.d.) and was dubbed the "Snoopers' Charter".

Once your router has received the request from your mobile device or PC, it directs it to your ISP. They are the post office. ISPs have a huge number of servers, communications devices and cabling that connect your home to the Internet. Much like the mail carrier, your ISP needs and can see the destination address and your own address. The ISP makes sure your request is routed to its intended destination, regardless of where in the world the data exists and what cables or satellites are used to get there.

Typically, your ISP can't see the content of data being sent back and forth between you and the website you are accessing, but this does depend on the type of protocol in use. Today, the vast majority of Internet traffic is encrypted, which means that anyone on the Internet monitoring network traffic can only see the source and destination addresses; they don't know what specific pages of a website you have visited nor the content of any forms you've completed, or searches submitted. What they can see is the destination domain as well as the source IP address. In the same way, anyone handling your letter passing through the postal service can see the destination and return address written on the back. Some advanced hacking techniques can give visibility to all of that data. Still, these require people to connect their devices to untrusted networks or, in extreme cases, state-level efforts to compromise large portions of the Internet, commonly known as "man-in-the-middle" attacks; however, both are difficult to do and therefore rare.

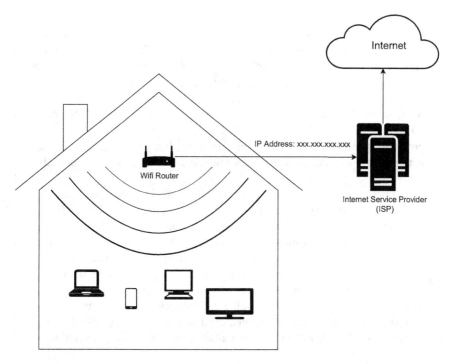

Figure 1.2 Home WiFi network.

Once the requests have found their way across the Internet to the destination server that holds the website or data, it will interpret the request and reply to you. The reply follows a similar route all the way back to you. All of this happens within milliseconds, hundreds of times per second for every page you access, email received, files downloaded or videos streamed. See Figure 1.2 for a visual representation of this process as a whole.

Psychological considerations: The role of legal pornography

Before we go on to discuss ways that people might commit sexual offences or engage in risky behaviour online, it is worth considering the influence of legal pornography. You may be working with someone whose pathway into online offending began with legal pornography, or it may be that they have developed a reliance on/addiction to pornography alongside offending behaviour representing a pattern of hypersexual behaviour. But what is the influence of this "legal" pornography having?

For the last ten years, a well-known pornography hosting website "Pornhub" has been releasing annual statistics about their users and the content that is being accessed, and these statistics shed interesting light on what is considered mainstream pornography. Worldwide in 2023 the most searched for term was 'hentai' (see Chapter 2 for a glossary of anime-related terms), which Pornhub state has held the top spot for three years in a row, suggesting a developing interest in non-photographic pornographic imagery.

What might we be concerned about with this growing interest? Hentai pornography is "rife with graphic sexual violence" (p. 2; Dines & Sanchez, 2023) and the British Board of Film Classification (BBFC) report that hentai promotes "an interest in abusive relationships". For example, in their 2023 paper, Gail Dines and Mandy Sanchez note that in their search of Pornhub:

> A quick search of the site can readily find pornified videos of Toy Story, Zootopia, Harry Potter, Sailor Moon, Elsa from Frozen, The Little Mermaid, Dora the Explorer, and My Little Pony. In recent years, too, other popular search terms and categories listed on Pornhub's yearly reviews, which may well attract the interests of minors and predators alike, have included "gamer girl", "babysitter", "cosplay", "school girl", "father-daughter", and "bratty sis". The site also features female teens tagged as "small", "exxxtra small", and "innocent", as well as "runaway", "homeless" and "abandoned". All of these videos represent violent, often illegal, and nonconsensual sex as desirable, and pleasurable.
>
> (p. 2)

The fact that hentai is non-photographic does of course mean that there is no identified victim within the images. However, the sexualisation of vulnerable groups in this way could contribute to the development of powerful distorted views about what is 'normal' or 'ok' in pornography/sex (see Chapter 3 on cognitive distortions common to those who offend online). Indeed, Steel et al. (2021) found that adults who had possession of child abuse images viewed more hentai, 'teen'[1] porn and bestiality than those who did not offend.

Hentai is just one of many categories of concern within mainstream legal pornography. Well-known pornographic websites commonly advertise pornography under the category of 'teen' with a disclaimer that all models are 18+ however, the models are often depicted in a way that makes them appear youthful, naïve or sometimes vulnerable. These legal pornography sites also host material depicting 'step' relationships, e.g. stepbrother, stepsister and stepmother, which some might also consider problematic.

A person's experience of legal pornography, when it comes to understanding online sexual offending, is important to consider as an assessor; many of the people we assess might have begun to normalise the sexualisation of young people, sometimes in sudo-incestuous relationships, prior to their behaviour escalating to offending. Additionally, whilst the Internet may be a place for potential online offenders to meet an existing deviant interest, many believe that the availability of the above types of pornographic images is crystalising those interests in individuals with no pre-existing sexual deviances (e.g. Wood, 2013).

> Now that you have an understanding of how the Internet works, we will look at ways that people might commit online offences in Chapter 2.

Note

1 The term 'teen porn' is an ambiguous term which clinically should be avoided. Whilst 'teen' could refer to legal images of people aged 18 and 19, it is sometimes used interchangeably with the term 'child porn' to reference indecent images of children. In the UK, the term 'child porn' is outlawed (Interagency Working Group on Sexual Exploitation of Children, 2016) to avoid trivialising the sexual abuse of children.

References

Barnes, L., & Mackie, P. (2022, January 19). *Ben John: Extremist ordered to read books is jailed*. BBC. Retrieved February 25, 2024, from https://www.bbc.co.uk/news/uk-england-leicestershire-60051861

Weaving the Web: The past, present and future of the world wide web by its inventor. London: Orion Business.

British Board of Film Classification. (2002, December 6). New BBFC research reveals children are more exposed to sites specializing in non-photographic pornography, compared to adults. Retrieved July 28, 2024 from https://www.bbfc.co.uk/about-us/news/new-bbfc-research-reveals-children-are-more-exposed-to-sites-specialising-in-non-photographic-pornography-compared-to-adults

Couldry, N. (2012). *Media, society, world: Social theory and digital media practice.* Cambridge: Polity Press.

Dines, G., & Sanchez, M. (2023). Hentai and the pornification of childhood: How the porn industry just made the case for regulation. *A Journal of Analysis of Exploitation of Violence, 8*(1). https://doi.org/10.23860/dignity.2023.08.01.03

Dokoupil, T., Charles, J., Toney, H. M., Russell, N., Lambers, W., Gfoeller, M., & Depetris, D. R. (2011, February 21). *Sorry about all the bombs*. Newsweek. Retrieved February 25, 2024, from https://www.newsweek.com/sorry-about-all-bombs-68549

Interagency Working Group on Sexual Exploitation of Children. (2016). *Terminology Guidelines for the protection of children from sexual exploitation and sexual abuse.* Retrieved 17th September 2024 from https://www.interpol.int/en/Crimes/Crimes-against-children/Appropriate-terminology

Investigatory Powers Act 2016. (2016). *Investigatory Powers Act 2016*. Retrieved March 3, 2024, from https://www.legislation.gov.uk/ukpga/2016/25/contents/enacted

Petrosyan, A. (2024, January 31). *Internet and social media users in the world 2024*. Statista. Retrieved February 24, 2024, from https://www.statista.com/statistics/617136/digital-population-worldwide/

Taylor, P. (2023, November 16). *Data growth worldwide 2010–2025*. Statista. Retrieved February 17, 2024, from https://www.statista.com/statistics/871513/worldwide-data-created/

Total number of Websites. (n.d.). *Internet live stats*. Retrieved February 25, 2024, from https://www.internetlivestats.com/total-number-of-websites/

Wood, H. (2013). Internet pornography and paedophilia. *Psychoanalytic Psychotherapy, 27*(4), 319–338. https://doi.org/10.1080/02668734.2013.847851

2 Online sexual offending and online harm

Christopher Wise and Jennifer Bamford

Introduction

One of the challenges we faced while writing this book was defining the types of offences committed online and reconciling the various terms and labels applied to those crimes. As discussed in the Introductory chapter, this book aims to cover the most prevalent and impactful of online offences. In this chapter, we will look specifically at online child sexual offences, online sexual offences and online harms.

Online child sexual offences

Indecent images of children

The rise of indecent images of children (IIOC) is a problematic trend closely tied to the growth of the Internet; it was in 1996 that the UK Metropolitan Police approached the Internet Service Providers' Association (ISPA), raising concerns that Newsgroups (an early messaging system where users could post images, files and text) contained illegal images. Chief Inspector Stephen French wrote an open letter to the ISPA asking that a list of over 130 Newsgroups be banned and that the Police's view was that they effectively believed the ISPs were guilty of publishing indecent images (Brown, 2017). Because of these matters, the Internet Watch Foundation (IWF; originally known as the Safety Net Foundation) was created. We will look at some of the positive efforts being undertaken by this organisation in later chapters.

At the time of the IWF's creation in 1996, 18% of the world's child sexual abuse imagery was hosted in the UK (Internet Watch Foundation, n.d.). In Chapter 6, we will delve deeper into the details and complexities of the law surrounding online offences. For now, we will touch on some of the different offences that can be committed and their technical differences.

UK law distinguishes between three types of offences: 'possessing', 'making' and 'distributing' indecent images of children. 'Making' may read as requiring a perpetrator to have taken or created the image, but this is not the case; accessing a website without actively downloading and saving the image is considered making if it is saved in a local cache by the internet browser, or even just displayed

DOI: 10.4324/9781003543794-2

on the screen. According to the Crown Prosecution Service's legal guidance on possession of indecent images (Crown Prosecution Service, 2018), deleting an indecent image is sufficient in most cases to divulge the offender of having possession of the image; however, they would still be guilty of *making* the image. For a thorough breakdown of these distinctions, please see Chapter 6.

While there have been ongoing and highly effective campaigns to remove indecent images of children and take down the websites that host them, the methods and technologies used by those who offend online have grown more complex and sophisticated to stay one step ahead of law enforcement and activist organisations such as the IWF and WeProtect Global Alliance. We will discuss this more in Chapters 4 and 8.

One of the most concerning trends in online image offending is that recent figures from the IWF have revealed that 90% of the images it had identified and removed from websites were self-generated[1] and produced through coercion and grooming (Hern, 2024).

Non-photographic indecent images of children

This form of indecent imagery is generally associated with Hentai/Lolicon, a sub-genre of Japanese manga and anime cartoons or comics featuring overly sexualised characters, including depictions of children. Internationally, the legality of this material differs substantially between countries. In Brazil, no crime has been committed if no actual child is depicted, regardless of the realism or explicitness of the imagery. However, within the UK, Section 62 of the Coroners and Justice Act 2009 made it an offence to possess a prohibited image of a child. This law specifically targets computer-generated imagery (CGI), cartoons and manga images. Additionally, the Crown Prosecution Service guidelines suggest that if a CGI image is realistic and of a high enough quality to look like a photograph or pseudo-photograph, it should be prosecuted as such.

Clinical considerations: If you're working with someone who has accessed Japanese 'manga', the following terms (which is not an exhaustive list) might be helpful for you to be familiar with:

Anime: A style of Japanese film and television animation, typically aimed at adults as well as children.
Manga: Means 'undisciplined words' in Japanese referring to art as a form of entertainment. Manga pornography is just one small percentage of manga. *Kodomo manga* is a type of manga which is for children. *Shonen manga* is for boys aged 12–18. *Shoujo manga* is for girls aged 12–18. *Josei manga* is for adult women above the age of 20. *Seinen manga* is for young men aged 18–30.

Hentai manga: A pornographic, adult manga. Hentai means 'pervert' in Japanese.

Ecchi: A genre in Japanese anime and manga that refers to erotic but not sexual content. It may include partial nudity, including nipples, but never exposed genitals. *Ero manga/ero anime* is another name for erotic manga.

Urotsukidoji: Anime including scenes of violence, rape and sadomasochism, most popular for its depiction of tentacle rape.

Doujinshi: A self-published amateur derivative artwork.

Guro: Called 'Ero Guro', often shortened to Guro, refers to a Japanese art form that is bizarre, gory or involves mutilation combined with eroticism. Gory Hentai is often referred to as Guro if, for example, the images depict missing limbs, blood or spilling organs.

Netorare: A genre of anime, manga or video game focused on infidelity. Commonly a subgenre of pornographic Hentai anime, netorare storylines typically focus on the internal distress caused by one member in a relationship cheating on the other.

Communication offences

Communication offences may include adults engaging in inappropriate discussions with children online or also involve adults discussing with one another about the abuse of children or encouraging each other to abuse children.

With the rise of social media and, in particular, its popularity with young people and children, the ease with which online offenders can communicate, sometimes anonymously, with children has grown significantly. It was only in 2017 that the UK government passed specific legislation to protect children from sexual communication. Despite this law coming into effect, there has been an increase of 82% in online grooming, with 73% of crimes linked to Snapchat and Meta (Formerly Facebook; NSPCC, 2023). Websites, such as Omegle, have been thought to have contributed to the opportunity for adults to engage in sexual communication with children. Omegle was a website that allowed users free access to the site without registering (see Chapter 4 for the results of a study on the cognitive distortions of Omegle users). Users would be randomly paired with other users in one-on-one chat sessions. The website was shut down in 2023 following a $22 million lawsuit filed in 2019 over a user who became a victim of child sexual exploitation.

Online sexual offences

Extreme imagery

Other forms of illegal images include those deemed as "extreme"; this includes bestiality, so-called "snuff" films (a pornographic film or video recording of an actual murder), necrophilia and rape. Following the murder of schoolteacher

Jane Longhurst in 2003, her mother, Liz Longhurst, campaigned for extreme pornography to be made illegal. During the trial of Jane Longhurt's murderer, Graham Coutts, violent internet pornography was implicated (Roberts, 2006). This campaign led to new legislation in the form of Section 63 of the Criminal Justice and Immigration Act 2008, which made possession of such imagery an offence.

Clinical considerations: Clinically, we often see clients who have charges/convictions for both possession of indecent images of children and other extreme images. It is helpful in understanding the reason for their offending, to try to discern between these categories and to discuss related but possibly dissimilar motivations. Considerations might include:

– *Has your client only sought out images of children, which may indicate a very specific interest, or was their online behaviour broader?*
– *What was the ratio of their use of legal pornography/indecent images of children/other extreme images? (a client may not always be honest here, and having a forensic report, if available, can be useful).*
– *If accessing extreme images, what were common themes? Bestiality, violence, etc.*
– *Were they also seeking out non-sexual extreme images, e.g. 'gore'. If so, what was this meeting for them? Was it about sexual arousal or other motivations, such as psychological arousal/shock?*

Intimate image abuse

Often inappropriately termed as "Revenge Porn", the non-consensual sharing of intimate images via either websites, social media, email or chat tools is not a new phenomenon. The scenario most people envision involves a former partner sharing images to cause embarrassment or distress to victims following the breakdown of a relationship; however, this type of offence may also be perpetrated by those looking to make financial gain from the sharing of pornographic images without necessarily a vengeful intent. Within England and Wales, this is an offence under Section 33 of the Criminal Justice and Court Act 2015, punishable by up to two years in prison. In addition, this offence was made a priority under the Online Safety Act, requiring technology companies to prevent and remove this illegal material from their services proactively.

Children can also be victims of this form of online sexual offence where images have been shared within a consensual, age-appropriate relationship.

Pornographic deepfakes

Deepfakes present a terrifying societal risk. Given that the first example of a deepfake was pornographic, it is unsurprising that the technology has continued to be used for this purpose, only growing in volume, sophistication and availability. Several adult websites exist solely to host, create and distribute deepfake videos of celebrities; this mostly goes unpoliced due to the paucity of countries with legislation protecting victims from this form of offending.

A form of intimate image abuse or non-consensual pornography involves the use of deepfake technology that can take an image and remove the clothing from the person in it; several websites on the clear and dark web offer this service for free with a delay and watermark, or priced per hundred images. Alarmingly, some well-known websites used for hosting coding projects, such as GitHub.com, allow anyone to download the source code used in these websites, allowing more technically capable individuals to run this deepfake software themselves. The recent Online Safety Act introduced within the UK takes a first step at combatting both intimate image abuse and pornographic deepfake technology (Hern, 2022).

An area of particular concern is the use of artificial intelligence (AI) in the production of deepfake child sexual abuse material. Whereas traditional deepfakes have involved overlaying a person's face over another, the recent advancements in AI image and video production have made it possible to teach an AI to produce realistic pictures and videos from text-based prompts. The IWF has reported a significant increase in both the volume and sophistication of this use of deepfake technology, including the use of AI to create new child abuse material for existing victims. In some cases, these images have been of greater severity, further highlighting the technological advancements in AI's negative uses (Internet Watch Foundation, 2024). For more information about AI, what it is and how it is being misused, we explore this in Chapter 3.

Cybersex trafficking

Cybersex trafficking or technology-facilitated sex trafficking describes the use of the Internet and related software and technologies to traffic. Victims are predominantly women and children, and they are transported to "cybersex dens", where there are webcams that record and stream their abuse. Recent statistics indicate that 40% of trafficking victims are recruited online (United Nations, 2021). Due to the technological nature of this form of trafficking, as opposed to physical trafficking, these crimes create additional challenges for law enforcement and governments attempting to combat this form of online offending.

Cyber flashing

Cyber flashing, a form of sexual cyber violence, involves a person sending an unsolicited sexual image (e.g. of their genitals) to another person. This type of offence was until recently not considered an offence within the UK, and unsolicited "dick pics" were an odious experience for 40% of young women (Smith, 2018). In order for the Court to be satisfied that a cyber flashing offence has occurred, the perpetrator needs to intend to "cause alarm, distress or humiliation" or to be "reckless as to whether the recipient will be caused alarm, distress or humiliation". These are criteria likely to be easily met given the emotional impact that can be caused for victims of such a crime (Durán & Rodríguez, 2022).

Cyber flashing has been an offence since the introduction of Part 10 of the Online Safety Act, which took effect on 31st January 2024. The first person to be imprisoned for the offence of cyber flashing is Nicholas Hawkes, a registered sex offender who was convicted of two counts of cyber flashing and sentenced to 52 weeks for the offences (The Crown Prosecution Service, 2024). It is beyond the scope of this section to consider the psychological motivators for cyber flashing as a specific offence. However, recent research by McGlynn and Johnson (2021) suggests the motivations of "sexual gratification, a 'laugh', status building or homosexual bonding, boredom, reduced inhibitions, as an exercise of male power and entitlement and or harass, intimate control and distress" (p. 176).

Online harms

Cyberbullying and harassment

With the anonymity and reach that the Internet brings, bullying and harassment have become commonplace. Currently, within the UK, there is no legal definition of cyberbullying and, therefore, no specific laws that protect against it. Perpetrators of cyberbullying have been prosecuted under the Protection from Harassment Act 1997 (Anti-Bullying Alliance, n.d.).

The seriousness of cyberbullying should not be underestimated, and the impact on young people can be devastating. Statistics show that the percentage of adults and young people who have experienced cyberbullying is increasing; within the US, 64% of young adults (18–29) have experienced cyberbullying, and figures show that middle school-age children that have experienced cyberbullying are twice as likely to attempt suicide (Howarth, 2023).

Cyber extortion

Cyber extortion focuses on stealing and threatening to release sensitive data, unlike ransomware, which locks down and makes data inaccessible until a ransom is paid. Anyone can be a victim of cyber extortion, from individuals to multinational corporations and even governments. Attackers may threaten to release sensitive information or take down a website or computer system unless a ransom is paid.

Victims may not be aware that their information has been stolen, and in some cases, it may have been stolen from a third party. One of the most renowned cases of cyber extortion happened due to a hack and subsequent data breach of Ashley Madison's website in 2015. Ashley Madison is a commercial website that markets itself as facilitating extramarital affairs. The individual or group that committed the Ashley Madison hack called themselves "The Impact Team"; evidence suggests that this group was formed solely to hack Ashley Madison. They obtained several gigabytes of data, including customer names, email addresses, payment history, internal emails and other internal company data. In July 2015, the Impact

Team announced the hack and threatened to release the data if Ashley Madison's parent company, Avid Life Media, did not shut down the site and another similar site they owned. The data was released on the dark web for anyone to download a few days after the site showed no sign of shutting down. If the initial extortion of Ashley Madison was not bad enough, cyber extortionists began combing through the leaked data and began targeting individuals who had their data exposed (Krebs, 2015).

Technology-facilitated stalking

Technology-facilitated stalking, also known as cyberstalking, is a growing problem that can be as intrusive, threatening and frightening as in-person stalking. A recent study of victims of stalking within the US showed that nearly half of all in-person stalking victims were also subject to cyberstalking and that 80% of all victims of stalking were stalked using technology (U.S. Department of Justice, 2022).

Even as early as 2002, a commercial product called LoverSpy advertised its ability to "monitor and record the complete computer activity of a computer user" (p. 49; Fraser et al., 2010). For $89, its users could choose an e-greeting card that LoverSpy would send to the intended victim. When opened, it would download and install spyware. Ultimately, LoverSpy was taken down by the Federal Bureau of Investigation (FBI), and its creator was prosecuted (Fraser et al., 2010).

Kaspersky, a multinational cybersecurity company that provides antivirus and other security solutions to consumers and businesses, revealed that in 2023 it found 31,000 cases of "stalker ware" installed on mobile phone devices and that 40% of surveyed people worldwide stated that they had experienced or suspected that they had been stalked (Kaspersky, 2024). Kaspersky is also a co-founding member in the coalition against stalker ware – a collaboration between technology organisations and victim organisations (https://stopstalkerware.org/).

As these statistics show, stalkers commonly use technology as a tool, which makes sense given how much of our lives are now online and how it offers an easy way of surveilling a perpetrator's intended victim. Technology also provides several possible opportunities to track a person's movements, either through the use of stalker ware, which provides a real-time location through a mobile phone, or by placing an Apple AirTag or similar tracking device on a person or their vehicle. Despite Apple AirTags having anti-stalking features since they were released, there are still a large number of cases where stalkers are using the product to track their victims.

Should an AirTag be found to be following a person not linked to it, a notification is displayed on their phone warning them that an AirTag has been found moving with them, and the owner can see their location. Despite these protections, two stalking cases in the US resulted in murder directly linked to the use of Apple AirTags and at least 150 more reported cases; this led to a class-action lawsuit against Apple (Belanger, 2022). Similarly, within the UK, there have been several cases and successful prosecutions related to the use of AirTags in stalking, including a case in Swansea where the victim was notified via her phone that an AirTag was following her (Moore, 2022).

Additional considerations should be made to the advanced techniques that a technologically sophisticated stalker may use to offend (see Chapter 7 regarding forensic risk assessment and risk management with those who stalk). In particular, some types of attacks used to commit cybercrime could be utilised when cyberstalking. This might include social engineering, hacking, spear phishing and similar methods that could give the perpetrator access to personal email accounts, social media platforms or physical devices.

Promoting or encouraging psychological or physical harm

There are many forms of online harm. The Online Safety Act 2023 has created new legislation protecting the public and setting in law what protections online services need to put in place to prevent the spread of this illegal content. While some of the guidance is still in draft form, it aims to protect children from illegal and harmful content, including the following:

- Content that encourages, promotes or facilitates suicide, eating disorders and self-harm
- Epilepsy trolling
- Content that encourages dangerous stunts or challenges
- Content that depicts or encourages violence
- Abusive or hateful content
- Sending false information intending to cause non-trivial psychological or physical harm
- Threatening communications

Note

1 The term "self-generated" is used to describe child sexual abuse content that has been recorded using a webcam-enabled device such as a laptop, mobile phone, or tablet by the victim, not by an abuser. This may be as a result of coercion or sextortion, or non-coerced and instead created for social affirmation, or sexting within a consensual age-appropriate relationship. Terminology guidelines (Interagency Working Group on Sexual Exploitation of Children, 2016) recommend that the term "self generated" be used carefully to avoid implicitly or inadvertently placing blame on the child who has produced the content against their will.

References

Anti-Bullying Alliance. (n.d.). *Online bullying and the Law. Anti-Bullying Alliance.* Retrieved March 16, 2024, from https://anti-bullyingalliance.org.uk/tools-information/all-about-bullying/bullying-and-law/online-bullying-and-law

Belanger, A. (2022, December 6). Stalkers' "chilling" use of AirTags spurs class-action suit against Apple. *Ars Technica.* Retrieved August 18, 2024, from https://arstechnica.com/tech-policy/2022/12/apple-airtags-are-now-the-weapon-of-choice-for-stalkers-lawsuit-says/

Brown, J. (Ed.). (2017). *Online risk to children: Impact, protection and prevention.* Hoboken, NJ: Wiley.

Coroners and Justice Act 2009. (n.d.). *Coroners and Justice Act 2009*. https://www.legislation.gov.uk/ukpga/2009/25/section/62

The Crown Prosecution Service. (2018, December 20). *Indecent and prohibited images of children. The crown prosecution service*. Retrieved March 24, 2024, from https://www.cps.gov.uk/legal-guidance/indecent-and-prohibited-images-children

The Crown Prosecution Service. (2024, March 19). *Prison sentence in first cyberflashing case. The crown prosecution service*. Retrieved April 20, 2024, from https://www.cps.gov.uk/east-england/news/prison-sentence-first-cyberflashing-case

Data Protection Act 2018. (n.d.). *Data Protection Act 2018*. Retrieved March 9, 2024, from https://www.legislation.gov.uk/ukpga/2018/12/part/3/chapter/4/crossheading/obligations-relating-to-personal-data-breaches/enacted

Durán, M., & Rodríguez-Domínguez, C. (2022). Sending of unwanted dick pics as a modality of sexual cyber-violence: An exploratory study of its emotional impact and reactions in women. *Journal of Interpersonal Violence, 38*(5–6), 5236–5261.

Fraser, C., Olsen, E., Lee, K., Southworth, C., & Tucker, S. (2010, Fall). The new age of stalking: Technological implications for stalking. *Juvenile and Family Court Journal, 61*(4), 39–55. https://ipvtechbib.randhome.io/pdf/fraser2010.pdf

Hern, A. (2022, November 24). Online safety bill will criminalise 'downblousing' and 'deepfake' porn. *The Guardian*. https://www.theguardian.com/technology/2022/nov/24/online-safety-bill-to-return-to-parliament-next-month

Hern, A. (2024, January 16). Child sexual abuse: Self-generated imagery found in over 90% of removed webpages. *The Guardian*. https://www.theguardian.com/technology/2024/jan/17/child-sexual-abuse-self-generated-data-internet-watch-foundation-end-to-end-encryption

Howarth, J. (2023, November 22). 17 Cyberbullying facts & statistics (2024). *Exploding Topics*. Retrieved March 16, 2024, from https://explodingtopics.com/blog/cyberbullying-stats

Interagency Working Group on Sexual Exploitation of Children. (2016). Terminology Guidelines for the protection of children from sexual exploitation and sexual abuse. Retrieved 17th September 2024 from https://www.interpol.int/en/Crimes/Crimes-against-children/Appropriate-terminology

Internet Watch Foundation. (n.d.). *Our history. Internet watch foundation*. Retrieved March 24, 2024, from https://www.iwf.org.uk/about-us/why-we-exist/our-history/

Internet Watch Foundation. (2024, July). *What has changed in the AI CSAM landscape?* Retrieved September 17, 2024, from https://www.iwf.org.uk/media/nadlcb1z/iwf-ai-csam-report_update-public-jul24v13.pdf

Kaspersky. (2024, March 13). Global Kaspersky report reveals digital violence has increased. *Kaspersky*. Retrieved August 18, 2024, from https://www.kaspersky.com/about/press-releases/2024_global-kaspersky-report-reveals-digital-violence-has-increased

Krebs, B. (2015, August 21). Extortionists target Ashley Madison users – Krebs on security. *Krebs on Security*. Retrieved March 16, 2024, from https://krebsonsecurity.com/2015/08/extortionists-target-ashley-madison-users/

Madison, D. (2023, November 5). List: Here are the exams ChatGPT and GPT-4 have passed so far. *Business Insider*. Retrieved March 17, 2024, from https://www.businessinsider.com/list-here-are-the-exams-chatgpt-has-passed-so-far-2023-1?r=US&IR=T#chatgpt-passed-all-three-parts-of-the-united-states-medical-licensing-examination-within-a-comfortable-range-10

McGlynn, J., & Johnson, K. (2021). Criminalising cyberflashing: Options for law reform. *The Journal of Criminal Law, 85*(3), 171–188.

Moore, A. (2022, September 5). 'I didn't want it anywhere near me': How the Apple AirTag became a gift to stalkers. The Guardian. https://www.theguardian.com/technology/2022/sep/05/i-didnt-want-it-anywhere-near-me-how-the-apple-airtag-became-a-gift-to-stalkers

NSPCC. (2023, August 15). 82% rise in online grooming crimes against children in the last 5 years. *NSPCC*. Retrieved March 24, 2024, from https://www.nspcc.org.uk/about-us/news-opinion/2023/2023-08-14-82-rise-in-online-grooming-crimes-against-children-in-the-last-5-years/

Roberts, G. (2006, August 31). Bereaved mother's campaign leads to a ban on possession of violent porn. *The Independent*. https://www.independent.co.uk/news/uk/crime/bereaved-mother-s-campaign-leads-to-a-ban-on-possession-of-violent-porn-414107.html

Smith, M. (2018, November 19). Four in ten young women have been sent unsolicited sexual images. *YouGov*. Retrieved March 24, 2024, from https://yougov.co.uk/society/articles/21937-four-ten-young-women-have-been-sent-unsolicited-se

United Nations. (2021, October 30). Traffickers abusing online technology, UN crime prevention agency warns. *UN News*. Retrieved March 24, 2024, from https://news.un.org/en/story/2021/10/1104392

U.S. Department of Justice. (2022, 02). *Stalking victimization*, 2019. Bureau of justice statistics. Retrieved August 18, 2024, from https://bjs.ojp.gov/content/pub/pdf/sv19.pdf

3 Cybercrime

Christopher Wise and Jennifer Bamford

Introduction

This chapter explores various forms of cybercrime. Many topics discussed may be relevant to your work as a professional, but you may also be at risk of being the victim of some forms of cybercrime discussed herein. If you are worried about your online safety, please see Chapter 8 for valuable tips about keeping yourself safe online.

Hacking

What we now describe as hacking is the unauthorised access to a computer, network or website by a malicious person or organisation. In recent years, hacking has become synonymous with cybercrime. At its core, it involves breaking into someone's computer or network to access sensitive information, such as personal or financial information. Its origin in the 1950s and 1960s was much more innocent; computer science students at the Massachusetts Institute of Technology (MIT) used the term to describe a shortcut. Given the cost of running computers at the time, any programming shortcut saved time and money.

There are many different types of hacking, each with its own set of tools and techniques. It may come as a surprise, but one of the most effective techniques does not require any sophisticated computer skills or software – social engineering. This involves manipulating people to give access to their systems or information. Phishing is one of the most well-known forms of social engineering attack, and anyone with an email address will likely have seen it in action. We will delve into some of the sub-categories of hacking later in this chapter. In this section, we will speak more generally about approaches used by hackers to obtain access to computer systems or networks to steal data and disrupt businesses.

Television and film make it look relatively easy and exciting, but the reality is far from that. Hacking can be exceptionally time-consuming and monotonous, requiring a lot of patience and persistence. Hackers spend days, weeks and sometimes months attempting to identify vulnerabilities that they can exploit and use to circumvent security measures. In IT terms, a vulnerability is a security flaw in software or hardware that a malicious party can use to perform a destructive action on that software or hardware. There are many different vulnerability types and classifications, and

DOI: 10.4324/9781003543794-3

entire industries focus on identifying and protecting organisations from them, mine included. It is essential to understand that vulnerabilities exist in all devices, including mobile phones, computers, WiFi networks and smart devices. The most feared type of vulnerability is 'remote code execution (RCE)'. This type allows a hacker to run malicious code on an affected system, potentially enabling them to gain remote access. New vulnerabilities are discovered all the time, and there is a constant struggle between hackers and organisations to find and fix these flaws.

While the proposition of a hacker being able to gain access to your devices is entirely worrying, the average home user is not at much risk from a targeted attack. Hackers are much more likely to target businesses with far more ways to compromise their systems, and the reward will be much higher. That does not mean there is no risk; celebrities, politicians or business leaders should be concerned. The average home user is much more likely to become involved in a hacking attack via the breach of a business that holds their data; this could lead to personal or credit card information being posted on the dark web for sale. Within the UK, when an organisation is hacked, which leads to a loss of personal information, often referred to as a breach, they are legally obligated to report it to the Information Commissioner's Office (ICO) and to take all necessary steps to protect the impacted customers (Data Protection Act 2018, n.d.). The ICO also has the power to issue substantial fines where an organisation failed to protect customer data, the largest of which was for a British Airways (BA) breach in 2020. This breach resulted in the loss of data for 400,000 customers and went undetected for two months. For this breach, BA was fined £20m, the largest in the ICO's history, despite being substantially less than the £183m fine the ICO initially intended to issue (Tidy, 2020).

It is worth noting that, in most situations, forensic analysis of a "hacked" device will identify whether or not it has been hacked (see Chapter 3 for a breakdown of a digital forensic report).

Clinical considerations: You might have a client who tells you that they have been accused of online offences which they have not committed and that they were, instead, hacked. It might help you to understand more about them and their situation (and to assess the veracity of their claim) by thinking about/ asking them the following questions:

- *Why do you think you were hacked?*
- *Do you know anyone who would target you?*
- *Do you know anyone who has the skills to launch a hacking attack?*
- *Have you recently downloaded any software that could have been malicious? If so, what software?*
- *Has anyone else used your WiFi recently? Did you give them the password?*
- *Have you received any emails threatening you or blackmailing you?*

Phishing

One of the most prolific types of hacking is phishing; almost everyone with an email address is the target of this type of attack. As mentioned in the Hacking section, this form of social engineering aims to trick unsuspecting recipients into downloading files, clicking links and completing online web forms purporting to be from legitimate sources but instead are elaborate fakes. They take the form of emails or SMS messages, usually sent en masse to millions of email addresses and phone numbers worldwide. As you may have experienced, the quality of these phishing emails does vary, and while it does seem unlikely that anyone would be convinced of their legitimacy, within the United States alone, phishing is the most widely reported cybercrime with over 300,000 reported cases in 2022 (Petrosyan, 2023). While phishing is a sub-type of hacking, there are different categories of phishing; the list below is not exhaustive, but it includes the most effective and interesting.

Spear phishing

Instead of using generic messages and sending them to large numbers of people, this phishing method is targeted to a specific organisation or individual. The perpetrators will often use content crafted using publicly available information about the person or business. One of the most well-known attacks of this kind was perpetuated by the North Korean hacking group, the Lazarus Group, against Sony Pictures in 2014 (US Department of Justice, 2018). This hack resulted in the loss of internal emails, documents, unreleased films and the personal information of thousands of employees.

Vishing

Voice phishing is a type of social engineering that takes place over the phone. At its most rudimentary, attackers will pretend to be from a person's bank or other financial institution and try to get victims to provide their account information. More sophisticated vishing attacks have used voice cloning, a process whereby an artificial intelligence (AI) replicates a person's voice using samples. In 2020, an employee in a Japanese company received a call from a director whose voice they recognised, requesting that they transfer $33 million to pay for a new acquisition the company was making. Unbeknownst to them, this was an elaborate vishing attack, and they made the payment without questioning it; not only was this a very costly attack, but it was also the first occurrence of AI technology used as part of cybercrime (Brewster, 2017).

Whaling

Similar to spear phishing, this is a more targeted form of phishing; the difference is that it is even more targeted. It is directed at executives within an organisation, and the emails will contain personalised information about the targeted business or individual. They often convey a sense of urgency. Working within cybersecurity, we receive these types of emails and SMS messages regularly, usually claiming to be from the chief executive officer (CEO) and asking for us to reset a password, pay for a service or follow a link to a dangerous site on their behalf. These are not generic and will use our names, the name of the CEO, and other employees' details to make them seem legitimate. A prominent example of a whaling attack was in 2015, when cybercriminals had already compromised Mattel's computer network and diligently built an understanding of the corporate structure and procedures before launching their final whale phishing attack, costing Mattel $3 million.

Ransomware

Ransomware is a type of malicious software that, like other computer viruses, will attempt to spread itself to all computers on the same network once it has infected a computer. Once it has spread itself as far as possible, it will restrict access to the computer or files until a ransom is paid. Generally, ransomware attacks work by encrypting the files using a key known only to the cybercriminals behind the attack. Ransomware attacks have increased in frequency and severity in recent years due to the significant financial rewards that cybercriminals can extort from impacted organisations who are left with the choice of losing all of their data and undergoing the time-consuming and costly process of resetting everything back to day zero or paying the price to continue business as usual within hours. In either case, reputational damage to any organisation can have long-term repercussions due to loss of public trust.

The delivery method for ransomware can vary, either via using some of the phishing techniques we have already discussed or by exploiting a vulnerability. One of the most widely known ransomware attacks was named WannaCry; this global attack took place in May 2017 and exploited a vulnerability in the Microsoft Windows operating system. It encrypted data and demanded payment using Bitcoin. Bitcoin is a form of digital currency known as a cryptocurrency. Payments made using Bitcoin can be complicated to trace due to how cryptocurrencies work and their unregulated nature.

This attack was of particular interest because the exploit used to compromise machines made use of a vulnerability known and used by the US National Security Agency (NSA). The NSA had known about the vulnerability for several years but did not report it to Microsoft, which would have prevented them from using it for surveillance and intelligence-gathering purposes. It only notified Microsoft of the vulnerability when they realised that the details of the exploit had been stolen (Nakashima et al., 2017). In the one day it was active, WannaCry infected 230,000 computers in over 150 countries (Foxx, 2017). The UK's National Health Service (NHS) was brought to a standstill for several days, and thousands of appointments were cancelled (National Audit Office, 2017).

Identity theft

This type of online offending has evolved from an offline one. With the growth of the Internet, the availability and accessibility of personal information have only increased, as have the tools and techniques available to cybercriminals to obtain and share that information. Like its offline counterpart, cybercriminals will use a person's information to apply for credit cards and loans or even gain access to their bank accounts. The Internet has only made it easier for criminals to obtain that information and evade detection.

Identity theft can occur online in various ways, including phishing scams, malware attacks or data breaches of a business holding personal data, such as the British Airways attack we previously discussed. Massive datasets of compromised personal information are sold on the dark web on auction-style websites like eBay; the datasets that include financial information fetch the highest price and are quickly used to create fake credit applications or fraudulent purchases online. The repercussions for victims can be substantial, not only the incurred debts but also the damage to credit ratings. In some instances, online identity theft has led to a person's identity being used to engage in other types of crime or posting harmful content online.

An example of bulk identity theft occurred between 2012 and 2017. An employee in a US software company with access to personal information stole the data and wrote a unique piece of software to open PayPal accounts in the customers' names and apply for credit. During the five years that he was able to commit this fraud, he created approximately 8,000 accounts, and paid himself $3.5 million (US Attorney's Office, District of Nevada, 2018).

Online scams

While phishing is prevalent, it is not the only online offence targeted broadly at the general public. Here, we explore some of the other types of online scamming.

Romance scams

Recently, romance scams have made it into mainstream media through, for example, the Netflix dramatisation of the real-life "Tinder Swindler". Romance scams typically use fake social media or dating profiles and the illusion of a romantic or intimate relationship to manipulate or steal from victims. Examples of this type of manipulation include:

- Convincing the victim to make fake investments
- Paying for fictional medical expenses
- Paying for travel expenses to pay for a visit

While the case of the Tinder Swindler was one man exploiting a small number of high-net-worth women, the majority of cases are perpetrated by organised criminal gangs who operate scam centres in developing countries. In a recent case, one such centre used human trafficking to lure victims to perform scams en masse (Simonette & Ng, 2024). This is a growing form of online offending; the number of victims increased by a fifth in 2023 (Lloyds Banking Group, 2024). According to the research conducted by the British bank, men were most likely to fall victim to this type of scam, making up 52% of those affected, and the average amount stolen was £6,937 ($8,831).

Tech support scams

Tech support scams commonly take the form of a phone call or a pop-up in a web browser, purporting to be from the technical support division of a large software vendor, such as Microsoft. They claim that the victim's computer has a problem or that a virus has been detected. These scammers aim to gain remote access to the victim's computer. To get access, they talk the unsuspecting victim through the steps required to give them access; typically, this will be via installing specialist remote access software. Once they have access, they will attempt to steal data, install malware or perform a ransomware attack. In 2023, the US Federal Bureau of Investigation (FBI) reported that losses in the United States caused by tech support scams totalled over $924 million (Federal Bureau of Investigation, 2023).

Online shopping scams

Fake shopping websites

Frequently mimicking the look, layout and products found on popular online shopping sites, these clone websites will trick online shoppers into providing their credit card or banking information. In addition to potentially stealing this sensitive data, they will often harbour malware and attempt to infect visitors to the website. They are especially prevalent during well-known discount shopping events such as Black Friday and Cyber Monday.

Auction site scams

Both sellers and buyers on online auction sites like eBay or Facebook marketplace must be wary of scammers. These types of scams can involve selling items they do not have or purchasing items and then asking the seller to provide banking information to make payments.

Investment scams

These types of scams can be committed via phishing emails or, more commonly, since the rise of social media through fake profiles. Victims will often receive a direct message from a profile claiming to be from an expert investor promising they can help people make massive financial gains in so-called get-rich-quick schemes, usually in the form of cryptocurrency investment or stocks and share schemes. The scammer will offer to let them join a training scheme or invest money on their behalf.

Investment scamming is another type of online offending that has evolved from an offline one; pyramid, Ponzi or multi-level marketing schemes are still prevalent. In one such scheme, the IM Academy promises to teach fee-paying members to trade foreign exchange or cryptocurrencies successfully; instead, this is a cover for a pyramid scheme with members being brainwashed into recruiting additional victims rather than receiving the training as promised (EL PAÍS, 2022).

Artificial intelligence

Dark AIs

Before delving into the dark side of AI, let us establish what the term means. We are some way off the creation of human-like AI, so in current technological terms, when we talk about AI, we mean enabling a machine or system to sense, reason, act or adapt like a human. Recent developments in large language models (LLMs, a powerful type of AI system that is trained on large text datasets and can produce human-quality text, translations or creative content) have meant that sophisticated chatbots such as OpenAI's ChatGPT are now available for everyone; these tools are powerful and represent a considerable step up in the practical application of AI technologies. The availability and power of these tools represent new challenges and risks for society. The EU is leading the way in establishing new regulatory standards to understand and assess the risks posed by AI platforms and services (European Commission, 2024).

To give an example of what an LLM can produce, I asked Google's Gemini AI the following prompt: "write a paragraph to describe what future capabilities an AI like yourself might have". This was the response:

> *Future AI models like myself hold the potential for remarkable advance-ments. We may become increasingly adept at understanding and responding to complex, nuanced instructions, tailoring responses to individual users and their contexts. The ability to learn and adapt quickly might enable us to assist with research, summarize vast information stores, and even provide insights that humans would struggle to find. We might seamlessly integrate with other AI tools, collaborating to solve intricate problems in fields like medicine, engineering, and environmental science. However, crucial to this progress is the continued focus on responsible development - ensuring fairness, trans-parency, and the mitigation of potential biases is crucial for AI to truly serve society in a positive, inclusive manner.*

As you can imagine, if AI services built for the everyday consumer require new legislation to understand and monitor the risk to society, what happens when cyber-criminals develop their *dark* versions?

This has already happened. The first, WormGPT, was announced on underground markets and forums in July 2023. The developers of ChatGPT released it with protections that make it very difficult to use for anything it deems illegal or malicious. While there have been successful attempts to circumvent these controls, OpenAI is constantly increasing the security, ethical and protective controls it has in place. On the other hand, WormGPT and the other dark AI that have become available to purchase do not have these protections. Instead, they are sold to provide more sophisticated means for cybercriminals to offend online. This leads to the question of what these tools are capable of and how cybercriminals will use them.

Malware and malicious code: Chatbots like ChatGPT and its dark equivalents can answer questions written in natural language with high accuracy; one such use is as a software coding assistant. For example, a cybercriminal could ask ChatGPT to write the code for a ransomware application. ChatGPT would identify this as illegal and refuse to generate the code. However, its dark AI cousin would write it. The ability to generate working code without requiring much technical experience in writing software makes it substantially easier for non-technical criminals to start to commit online offences.

Improved phishing capabilities: One of the noticeable signs of phishing is poor spelling, grammar or other inaccuracies in the content of the email. Using a dark AI, a cybercriminal can produce higher-quality phishing emails by writing the initial email and reading and replying to any victim who responds to the attempt. This reduces the need for human involvement, increasing the number of phishing attacks a single offender can commit.

These are just two examples of how cybercriminals can use one type of dark AI. To put into perspective the potential dangers these pose, the most recent version of ChatGPT has passed the US Medical Licensing Examination and the US Bar exam, along with a host of other certifications (Madison, 2023). The current dark AIs have yet to reach this level of sophistication, but it is only a matter of time before they do. Dark AIs have also been implicated in online sexual offences, as we will discuss below.

Deepfakes

Deepfakes are highly realistic videos or audio recordings manipulated or created entirely using AI. They can make it appear like someone has said or done something they never did or create artificially generated illicit images. Indeed, the first deepfake created in 2017 was of the actress Gal Gadot's face superimposed on an existing pornographic video to make it appear as though the actress was engaged in the acts portrayed.

As discussed earlier in this chapter, vishing is one use for deep audio fakes; using this technology, it is possible to take a sample recording of someone's voice and create a digital version. Numerous legitimate websites offer this service for a small monthly fee, and while they have terms and conditions prohibiting using a person's voice without their permission, this is inevitably very difficult for the police to verify and prosecute, relying on victims reporting the misuse of the service. There are also dark web equivalents that offer both fake audio and video capabilities; these deepfake services offer to make videos ranging from $200 to $20,000 per minute, depending on the quality and purpose of the end product.

Examples of the type of uses mentioned include disinformation; whether political propaganda, fake news stories or misleading advertising, the consequences can be disastrous for public trust. One of the most alarming uses of this type of disinformation by governments was in 2023 when a pro-China *bot* (a software program that performs actions on the Internet) posted deepfake videos on Facebook and X (formerly Twitter) of artificially generated news anchors. These videos appeared to promote the interests of the Chinese Communist Party (Mozur, 2023). Another recent example of cyber fraud that used deepfake technology, which is still circulating today, is a purported video of Tesla CEO Elon Musk promoting cryptocurrency giveaways (Tidy, 2022).

Cyberterrorism

The term "cyberterrorism" was first coined in the 1990s by Barry Collin, who described it as "CyberTerrorism attacks us at the point at which the 'physical world' and 'virtual world' converge" (Collin, 1997). However, there are varying opinions on the definition and use of the term, with some considering it overused and a form of media exaggeration. To date, there has never been a cyberattack that has directly resulted in a loss of life; indirectly, however, ransomware attacks against hospitals have resulted in deaths (Perlroth, 2020), but none of these have been attributed to a known terrorist organisation.

Suppose we extend the term to include non-fatal cyberattacks orchestrated by terrorist organisations. In that case, some notable examples include one such attack on X (formerly Twitter) and *The New York Times*, where they lost control of their websites due to a targeted attack by a pro-Syrian government organisation (Reuters, 2013).

The majority of Internet usage by terrorist organisations is centred around recruitment, radicalisation and propaganda. There have also been occurrences where intelligence services have hacked the terrorists; in 2011, MI6 successfully hacked an al-Qaeda online magazine, where they replaced bomb-making instructions with a recipe for a cupcake (Gardham et al., 2011).

How online offending is changing

As the examples above show, numerous, ever-changing and complex ways to offend online exist. As technology continues to evolve and we become more online as a society, cybercriminals will inevitably find more ways to exploit those systems and us. The rise of AI, in particular, presents a genuine threat to our society, and the upcoming legislation regarding its use (European Parliament, 2023) is essential to creating safeguards. However, what is being done about the emerging AI threats within the dark web? They are several steps behind their legitimate counterparts' capabilities, but this new technology is constantly improving. Law enforcement and governments need to start planning for this inevitable step change in the capabilities of cybercriminals and the tools they have available to them.

In Chapter 4, we will explore some ways in which online offenders get caught.

References

Brewster, T. (2017, November 9). Fraudsters cloned company director's voice in $35 million heist, *Police Find. forbes.com.* Retrieved March 9, 2024, from https://www.forbes.com/sites/thomasbrewster/2021/10/14/huge-bank-fraud-uses-deep-fake-voice-tech-to-steal-millions/?sh=2d7688947559

Collin, B. (1997, 03). Future of cyberterrorism. *Crime and Justice International, 13*(2), 15–18. https://www.ojp.gov/ncjrs/virtual-library/abstracts/future-cyberterrorism-physical-and-virtual-worlds-converge

EL PAÍS. (2022, April 18). Families in despair over IM Academy: 'The crypto-sect has kidnapped our children'. *EL PAÍS English.* https://english.elpais.com/international/2022-04-18/families-in-despair-over-im-academy-the-crypto-sect-has-kidnapped-our-children.html#

European Commission. (2024, March 6). AI Act | Shaping Europe's digital future. *Shaping Europe's Digital Future.* Retrieved March 16, 2024, from https://digital-strategy.ec.europa.eu/en/policies/regulatory-framework-ai

European Parliament. (2023, June 8). EU AI Act: First regulation on artificial intelligence | topics. *European Parliament.* Retrieved April 20, 2024, from https://www.europarl.europa.eu/topics/en/article/20230601STO93804/eu-ai-act-first-regulation-on-artificial-intelligence

Federal Bureau of Investigation. (2023). *Internet Crime Report 2023.* https://www.ic3.gov/Media/PDF/AnnualReport/2023_IC3Report.pdf

Foxx, C. (2017, May 13). Cyber-attack: Europol says it was unprecedented in scale. *BBC.* https://www.bbc.co.uk/news/world-europe-39907965

Gardham, D., Wallace, S., Furness, H., Kilner, J., Brown, O., & Coles, B. (2011, June 2). MI6 attacks al-Qaeda in 'Operation Cupcake'. *The Telegraph.* https://www.telegraph.co.uk/news/uknews/terrorism-in-the-uk/8553366/MI6-attacks-al-Qaeda-in-Operation-Cupcake.html

Lloyds Banking Group. (2024, February 2). Romance scams rose by a fifth in 2023. *Lloyds Banking Group.* Retrieved March 16, 2024, from https://www.lloydsbankinggroup.com/media/press-releases/2024/lloyds-bank-2024/romance-scams-rose-by-a-fifth-in-2023.html

Madison, D. (2023, November 5). List: Here are the exams ChatGPT and GPT-4 have passed so far. *Business Insider.* Retrieved March 17, 2024, from https://www.businessinsider.com/list-here-are-the-exams-chatgpt-has-passed-so-far-2023-1?r=US&IR=T#chatgpt-passed-all-three-parts-of-the-united-states-medical-licensing-examination-within-a-comfortable-range-10

Mozur, P. (2023, February 7). How deepfake videos are used to spread disinformation. *The New York Times.* https://www.nytimes.com/2023/02/07/technology/artificial-intelligence-training-deepfake.html

Nakashima, E., Timberg, C., & Semansky, P. (2017, May 16). NSA officials worried about the day its potent hacking tool would get loose. *Then It Did. Washington Post.* https://www.washingtonpost.com/business/technology/nsa-officials-worried-about-the-day-its-potent-hacking-tool-would-get-loose-then-it-did/2017/05/16/50670b16-3978-11e7-a058-ddbb23c75d82_story.html

National Audit Office. (2017, October 27). Investigation: WannaCry cyber attack and the NHS - NAO report. *National Audit Office*. Retrieved March 10, 2024, from https://www.nao.org.uk/reports/investigation-wannacry-cyber-attack-and-the-nhs/

Perlroth, N. (2020, September 18). Cyber attack suspected in German woman's death. *The New York Times*. https://www.nytimes.com/2020/09/18/world/europe/cyber-attack-germany-ransomeware-death.html

Petrosyan, A. (2023, August 29). U.S. most frequently reported cyber crime by number of victims 2022. *Statista*. Retrieved March 9, 2024, from https://www.statista.com/statistics/184083/commonly-reported-types-of-cyber-crime-us/

Reuters. (2013, August 28). New York Times, Twitter hacked by Syrian group. *The Daily Star*. https://www.thedailystar.net/news/new-york-times-twitter-hacked-by-syrian-group

Simonette, V., & Ng, K. (2024, March 14). Hundreds rescued from love scam centre in the Philippines. *bbc.co.uk*. https://www.bbc.co.uk/news/world-asia-68562643

Tidy, J. (2020, October 16). British airways fined £20m over data breach. *BBC*. Retrieved March 9, 2024, from https://www.bbc.co.uk/news/technology-54568784

Tidy, J. (2022, June 10). YouTube accused of not tackling Musk Bitcoin scam streams. *BBC*. https://www.bbc.co.uk/news/technology-61749120

U.S. Attorney's Office, District of Nevada. (2018, July 30). Reno man sentenced to four years in prison for creating over 8000 fraudulent online accounts with stolen identities to commit $3.5 million fraud scheme. *Department of Justice*. Retrieved March 10, 2024, from https://www.justice.gov/usao-nv/pr/reno-man-sentenced-four-years-prison-creating-over-8000-fraudulent-online-accounts-stolen

US Department of Justice. (2018, September 6). North Korean regime-backed programmer charged with conspiracy to conduct multiple cyber attacks and intrusions. *Department of Justice*. Retrieved March 9, 2024, from https://www.justice.gov/opa/pr/north-korean-regime-backed-programmer-charged-conspiracy-conduct-multiple-cyber-attacks-and

U.S. Department of Justice. (2022, 02). *Stalking Victimization*, 2019. Bureau of Justice Statistics. Retrieved August 18, 2024, from https://bjs.ojp.gov/content/pub/pdf/sv19.pdf

4 How online offenders are tracked and apprehended

Christopher Wise and Jennifer Bamford

Introduction

Now that we understand the technologies and techniques online offenders use to offend online, we will look at some of the excellent work undertaken by police forces, government agencies and other organisations to tackle the ever-evolving landscape of online offending.

It is important to note that this chapter is not an exhaustive list of the agencies working to tackle online crime. We have chosen to describe some key contributors to this critical area of law enforcement. We will also explore some of the technical aspects that lead to the detection and arrest of online offenders.

As discussed in the Introductory chapter, cybercrime is viewed as a national security problem, whereas other online offences and harm are public safety issues. This difference is often reflected in the focus of the organisations discussed in this chapter, where they will focus on one or the other, or sometimes both.

Psychological/therapist considerations: Sometimes, when working with a client arrested or convicted for online offending, you may have information in court or police documents about the agency that apprehended them. This chapter is to help you understand more about those agencies.

UK National Crime Agency

The UK National Crime Agency (NCA) was founded in 2013 in an attempt by the then UK Home Secretary, Teresa May, to create a more unified organisation to tackle and fight organised crime. The NCA has been described as the UK's equivalent of the US Federal Bureau of Investigation (FBI). It houses several units focusing on serious and organised rime (SOC), terrorism and several units explicitly dedicated to cybercrime and online sexual offending:

National Cyber Crime Unit

The National Cyber Crime Unit (NCCU) focuses on critical cyber incidents in the UK and targets the online tools and services criminals use to communicate and commit cybercrimes.

DOI: 10.4324/9781003543794-4

Child Exploitation and Online Protection Command

The Child Exploitation and Online Protection (CEOP) was formed in 2006 before merging with the NCA in 2013. Since its inception, the purpose of the CEOP has been to bring child sex offenders to the UK courts by working in partnership with national and international organisations, both governmental and private.

Joint Operations Cell

The Joint Operations Cell (JOC) is a collaborative effort by the Government Communications Headquarters (GCHQ) and the NCA created in 2015 specifically to target crimes being committed on the dark web, including child sexual exploitation, sex trafficking and the sale of drugs and weapons on the dark web marketplaces.

Since its inception, the NCA has been tackling cybercrime as a core part of its purpose. It has been responsible for many large-scale arrests, assisted UK police forces and collaborated with international agencies.

National Cyber Security Centre

Acting primarily in an advisory capacity, the National Cyber Security Centre (NCSC) is an arm of GCHQ that supports the UK public and private sectors and the general public. It provides practical guidance to help organisations and individuals protect themselves online and reduce the risk of becoming victims of cybercrime. For the most damaging cyberattacks, it will also provide incident response.

International cybercrime agencies

Interpol

Interpol has a dedicated division that monitors and reports on changes and trends in cybercrime; starting in 2014, the Cyber Fusion Centre brings together experts from industry and law enforcement to analyse crime across the Internet and provide actionable intelligence to countries. Interpol also runs operations globally targeting cybercrime, such as the African Joint Operation against Cybercrime (AFJOC).

In addition to their work on cybercrime, Interpol also has a unit dedicated to protecting children online, the Crimes Against Children unit. Its key aims include identifying and rescuing victims of sexual abuse, blocking access to child sexual abuse material (CSAM), and preventing offenders from travelling abroad to commit sexual offences or escape prosecution.

Bundeskriminalamt

Much like the British NCA, the Bundeskriminalamt (BKA) is the German equivalent of the FBI. As the central agency of the German police, it coordinates police activities that tackle cybercrime, online sexual offences and other illegal online harms. It has a division dedicated to this task called Division CC (Cybercrime).

European Cybercrime Centre

European Cybercrime Centre (EC3), created by Europol in 2013, was founded to strengthen the law enforcement response to cybercrime within the EU. Following its creation, EC3 recognised that due to the global nature of cybercrime, support from non-EU countries would be beneficial, and it launched the Joint Cybercrime Action Taskforce (J-CAT). These two organisations have contributed to high-profile operations, including Europol's Victim Identification Taskforce (VIDTF). Since its inception, the VIDTF has safeguarded over 533 children and led to the arrest of 182 offenders (Europol, 2021).

National Cyber Investigative Joint Task Force

Numerous agencies in the United States deal with cybercrime on some level, including the FBI, Department of Homeland Security (DHS), and even the US Coast Guard. The FBI established the National Cyber Investigative Joint Task Force (NCIJT), comprising over 30 partnering agencies across law enforcement and intelligence services to consolidate their efforts. It seeks to consolidate the capabilities of its contributing agencies to prevent and detect cybercrime.

Below, we will explore the work undertaken by the US agencies actively engaged in online offending globally.

US Department of Homeland Security

The DHS has been highly active in fighting online offending of all categories and has several dedicated subdivisions tasked with protecting the United States from cyber threats, including typical cybercrime targeting US citizens, protecting critical national infrastructure and preventing cyberterrorism. Following the enactment of the Homeland Security Act of 2002, the DHS began operations in March 2003, incorporating 22 agencies. Below, we will delve into some of the prominent agencies within the DHS that strongly focus on cybersecurity.

Cybersecurity and Infrastructure Security Agency (CISA): Like the UK NCSC, CISA works with domestic and international partner organisations in information exchanges, training, advising and analysing cyber threats. Unlike the NCSC, its remit extends beyond purely cybersecurity and includes the protection of critical national infrastructure. The agency started in 2007 as the DHS National Protection and Programs Directorate, becoming CISA in 2018 when its responsibilities grew to include securing elections.

US Secret Service (USSS): Commonly associated with the security of the President of the United States of America, the USSS is the first US agency to have permanent representation at Europol and is part of the J-CAT. The USSS is tasked with protecting the US financial infrastructure and creating a safe environment for US citizens to conduct financial transactions.

US Immigration and Customs Enforcement (ICE) – Homeland Security Investigations (HSI): This division of the DHS focuses on protecting against child exploitation. It is a founding member of the Virtual Global Task Force and the Crimes Against Children specialist working group created by Interpol. It also participates in the previously mentioned VIDTF. The HSI works globally, providing training and investigations across all aspects of cybercrime, including the dark web and cyber-enabled financial crime.

Operation Sunflower is an excellent example of the work conducted by the HSI, its Victim Identification Unit and the VIDTF. As part of Operation Sunflower, a cache of photos showing a girl no more than 11 years old looking out of the window of a vehicle travelling down a highway was found, with the caption for the image inviting viewers to submit suggestions on how best to sexually assault her and get away with it. The photos were discovered by Danish law enforcement on a chat board known to be frequented by those who commit harmful sexual behaviours. Using the blurred details in the photo, the HSI could narrow their search to Kansas, ultimately identifying the victim and prosecuting the would-be perpetrator (US Department of Homeland Security, 2022).

FBI – Internet Crime Complaint Center

The Internet Crime Complaint Center (IC3) is a division of the FBI tasked with gathering data on cybercrime and is where citizens or organisations can report a cybercrime.

Undercover police

As we will cover in Chapter 5, the number of criminals using the Internet to commit crimes and use the privacy and encryption tools available to hide is only increasing; in particular, the dark web poses a massive challenge to law enforcement agencies (LEAs). The use of undercover police, also known as covert policing, is one of the primary techniques we see being used to counter this growing trend. Covert policing is not a new approach, but online offenders' growing sophistication and technical knowledge create new challenges from a practical and legislative perspective.

An area of controversy surrounding undercover work is to what extent an undercover officer can engage in criminal activity to maintain their cover or gain the trust of the target criminals. Within the UK, the use of undercover officers and their use of criminal conduct to carry out their duties are covered by the Covert Human Intelligence Sources (Criminal Conduct) Act 2021. This bill caused some controversy but was ultimately passed into law (Amnesty International UK, 2020), permitting several bodies the capability to use not only undercover officers or covert sources but also the option to break the law. However, there are provisions within the act that prevent the use of criminal conduct if what is "sought" could be reasonably achieved "by other conduct which would not constitute a crime" (Covert Human Intelligence Sources (Criminal Conduct) Act 2021).

From our research, it is still being determined whether this relatively recent change in legislation has been used in the pursuit of online sexual offenders within the UK. However, one country where this type of legislation has been used to combat online offending is Australia, specifically Queensland's child exploitation unit, Task Force Argos. Task Force Argos has been at the centre of some of the most successful multinational investigations into the production and distribution of child sexual abuse material. In part, this success has been due to the Police Powers and Responsibilities Act 2000, which allows Queensland officers to apply for permission to share CSAM in the course of an undercover operation (Bleakley, 2019).

This re-sharing of CSAM material has some challenging ethical considerations, in particular the re-victimisation of children each time these images are shared online.

Undercover officers must develop, build and maintain online personas and, in some cases, perform illegal actions to gain access and the trust of online sexual offenders operating illegal websites and forums. Often, they will pose as offenders or children to lure people who are sexually offending online into engaging them in chats or image sharing. Officers sometimes impersonate the personas of online sexual offenders, mirroring their language and communication style. In the case of the dark web drug auction site the "Silk Road", a US LEA took control of the account of an administrator of the site during this operation. The officer was asked to take part in creating a new version of the Silk Road while law enforcement was taking over the site. This enabled them to capture contact information and addresses of online offenders who had used the site to purchase illegal substances.

One of the challenges in undercover operations is that criminals anticipate that officers are not permitted to commit criminal acts, and this also extends to online undercover operations. To gain access to websites or forums, new members must often share illicit images or stolen personal data, such as credit cards, to gain entry. One example is the dark website DarkMarket, which required prospective members to supply 100 stolen credit cards verified by two reviewers who vouch for their legitimacy (Lusthaus, 2018).

Cyber-vigilantism

In recent years, there has been increasing attention given to the use of cyber-vigilantism in online child abuse cases, otherwise known as 'paedophile hunters'. The aim of these groups is to patrol online spaces in search of those who intend to commit offences against children. They often do so via posing as children online and engaging with online offenders with the aim of arranging a time to meet; at this point, the individual will be apprehended, sometimes by the cyber-vigilante themselves, by the group they are affiliated with, and sometimes with the joint involvement of the police. The cyber-vigilantes often video record or live-stream the apprehension to bring public shame and identification to the alleged offender.

The use of cyber-vigilantism in detecting and prosecuting offenders is a complicated ethical and legal space. The police have raised concerns about the strategies used by vigilante groups which can prejudice investigations. However, there is also evidence of vigilante groups producing evidence to support prosecutions successfully (BBC News, 2019). In 2020, the Supreme Court ruled that paedophile hunters do not violate human rights (Sutherland v Her Majesty's Advocate, 2020). Furthermore, there is public support for cyber-vigilantism associated with a lack of confidence in the criminal justice system (Bateson, 2021).

In 2022, Anna Tippett conducted a study specifically exploring public perceptions of vigilante justice in the UK. From a survey of 102 individuals, the majority of respondents were supportive of the aims of cyber-vigilante groups, and there was expressed concern around the degree to which the criminal justice system could be relied upon to apprehend online offenders. However, respondents were also concerned about the shaming tactics used by vigilante groups, otherwise referred to as "doxing". Tippett concludes that *"there thus appears to be inconsistent agreement on what justice means more broadly, alongside confliction regarding what constitutes retribution in the digital age"* (p. 16).

Role of internet service providers and big tech

Internet service providers

Internet service providers (ISPs) are our gateways to the Internet and the digital world that resides within it. They connect individuals, businesses and organisations, creating the backbone that allows us to communicate and share data globally. ISPs occupy a unique position, and the data they have access to is crucial evidence that can lead to the identification and apprehension of people who offend online.

ISPs have a challenging role, balancing individuals' right to privacy with national security and public safety requirements. The UK legislation surrounding what data ISPs must track, retain and provide to the police is constantly changing. As the threat of cybercrime evolves, the need for ISPs to play a more significant part in capturing evidence and providing access to the police and intelligence services is constantly growing. The current legislation within the UK, as of 2024, requires ISPs to capture Internet Connection Records (ICR) and Communication Data (CD); this is the metadata around a communication, not the content itself. They record the user's or customer's identifier, source IP address, destination IP address or website visited. It is also possible for ISPs to include the length of time spent on the site or using the application and the volume of data transmitted.

It can be necessary to keep this data for a maximum of 12 months. As discussed in previous chapters, due to the extensive use of encryption when accessing websites or other internet-based services, ISPs have no access to content. ICR records do not contain the content, the details of the specific pages visited, or how a person used the website.

One of the drivers for making these changes to the regulations governing the retention of and access to CD was the loss of human intelligence, where, in the past, police and intelligence services could watch someone going to a bank or travel agent. These tasks moved online, creating a blind spot for LEAs.

Social media platforms

Social media platforms such as Facebook, X (formerly Twitter) and Snapchat have a complex and ever-evolving role in safeguarding children and preventing online crimes. While these platforms connect people and communities, criminals often exploit them. According to police figures obtained by the National Society for Prevention of Cruelty to Children (NSPCC, 2023), online grooming of children increased by 82%, and 73% of the crimes involved Snapchat and Meta-owned platforms (Instagram, Facebook, and WhatsApp).

While social media platforms are a prominent location for online sexual offenders to target children, these platforms are also used to commit a raft of other forms of online harm, including terrorism-related radicalisation, various forms of phishing, stalking and harassment, hate speech and identity theft (Drury et al., 2022).

Social media's anonymity and reach make identifying and prosecuting these offenders extremely complex. Social media companies have a moral and, increasingly, a legal responsibility to protect their users, particularly children. Unfortunately, there are some substantial challenges facing these organisations:

Reactive vs. Proactive: Social media platforms must balance protecting their user's civil liberties and privacy against their security and safety. As a result, action is typically only taken after harmful content has been posted. In recent years, substantial pressure has been placed on them to take a more proactive approach to blocking and removing dangerous content. During the US Senate Committee on the Judiciary hearing – "Big Tech and the Online Child Sexual Exploitation Crisis", the chief executive officers (CEOs) of the top five social media platforms spoke about the range of tools and approaches being used proactively to monitor and remove harmful content (Senate Committee on the Judiciary, 2024).

Scale: The sheer content volume on these platforms makes proactive moderation difficult. Social media platforms heavily rely on user reporting and increasingly on artificial intelligence (AI) tools that are only sometimes accurate. There have also been issues with human-based moderation and the impact on employees whose jobs are to view and moderate suspected harmful content. In 2020, Meta (formerly Facebook) paid 52 million dollars to employees working as content moderators who claimed that they had suffered severe mental health consequences as a result of viewing harmful content (Webber, 2020).

Encryption: End-to-end encryption (E2EE) in messaging services has become a standard expected by platform users. In Chapter 5, we will discuss the technicalities and legal challenges presented by this form of encryption in more depth. When E2EE is in use, these platforms cannot monitor message content for illegal or harmful content.

Legal and regulatory requirements

Several governments have enacted or are enacting new laws explicitly targeting social media companies and big tech to create a safer experience for users of these platforms and protect them from harm.

Online Safety Act (UK): With this act, the British government wanted "to make Britain the best place in the world to set up and run a digital business while simultaneously ensuring that Britain is the safest place in the world to be online". The Online Safety Act 2023 was passed into law, creating a regulatory framework for user-to-user services like Facebook and search engines like Google. It covers the protection of children and the removal of harmful content. It empowers the Office of Communications (Ofcom) to fine companies failing to meet these regulations up to £18 million or 10% of their global annual revenue, whichever is biggest.

EARN IT Act (US): The EARN IT Act of 2023 aims to amend Section 230 of the Communications Act 1934. Section 230, introduced in 1996, protects website operators from civil lawsuits arising from content posted on them. The bill would amend these protections and create a National Commission on Online Child Sexual Exploitation Prevention. This bill has yet to be passed into law and was initially proposed in 2020. Several privacy organisations have criticised the bill, citing concerns over encryption and privacy rights (Gross, 2020).

Network Enforcement Act – NetzDG (Germany): Known colloquially as the Facebook Act, it was passed into German law in 2017 and required that all social media platforms with over two million users remove "clearly" illegal content within 24 hours. This deadline is increased to seven days for content requiring additional review to determine its legality. The process for removal requires the platforms to have a transparent process for users to report harmful content. Due to the broad nature of the act and its high fines for failure to comply, it has drawn criticism within Germany and internationally. In 2017, David Kaye, the UN Special Rapporteur on the promotion and protection of the right to freedom of opinion and expression, wrote to the German government criticising the act with concerns that it is incompatible with human rights law (Kaye, 2017).

Cloud storage providers

Cloud storage services such as Google Drive, OneDrive and iCloud face similar challenges. In particular, balancing their user's right to privacy against identifying those who misuse their services for unlawful activity. A recent example of this challenge occurred when Google locked the account of a father who had been instructed to take photos of his son's groin to track the progress of an infection. He took the photos using his Android phone, and two days later, he received an email from Google stating that they had detected harmful content and that his account had been locked. By law, they were required to report this to the authorities. Even after the San Franciso Police Department determined no crime had occurred, Google refused to unlock the account (Schoon et al., 2022).

Apple caused controversy when it reneged on an initiative to detect child abuse images within its iCloud service. Initially announced in August 2021, by December 2022, they had reversed the decision, citing privacy and security concerns (Newman, 2023).

What Incognito means

The term "Incognito" describes a mode of operation for internet browsers that purportedly increases user privacy while using the browser. The feature was first released as part of the Chrome browser in 2008. Today, almost all browsers can open in Incognito mode or at least a similarly named option. While this feature does offer some additional privacy, this is only relevant in the case of shared devices (Porter, 2024). The idea behind the feature is that your browsing history is not visible to another user of that device, but this is as far as the protection goes. Your ISP, anyone snooping on your network activity, law enforcement agencies, and even your employer if you are using a corporate device will still be able to see what actions are being performed on that computer and recover the data associated with that browsing activity forensically.

Forensic report breakdown

Not all forensic reports look the same, but they generally contain the same type and level of information. Here, we will explore the key sections, give some examples of the data presented, and provide a non-technical explanation of what it means.

Exhibits Examined: Fairly self-explanatory, this section lists out the devices that have been forensically examined and a summary of the results, including which applications the evidence was discovered in.

Overview: Providing topline information on the devices, the overview includes any serial numbers, the operating systems and applications. In the case of mobile phones, this includes the International Mobile Equipment Identity number, a unique identifier for a phone. This also includes the details of the files found, their locations within the device and the application that uses that location, for example, WhatsApp. It also typically contains a table summarising the volume of evidence found. In the case of child sexual abuse material, there may be a table categorising the images and the number of each found.

You might notice that such a table contains 'accessible' and 'inaccessible' images/movies. The definition of inaccessible vs. accessible is touched upon within the Crown Prosecution Service's (CPS) legal guidance on Indecent and Prohibited Images of Children and could vary depending on the IT knowledge of the offender. For example, when a website is accessed, the content of that website is *cached* to the device; this is a local copy of all the images and pages that make up that website. If an offender were not aware of that cache, it would be considered "inaccessible". Similarly, if an offender deleted an image but it was recovered as part of the forensic analysis using specialist tools, the forensic analyst would also consider it to be inaccessible. However, the CPS guidance indicates that should the offender have "the wherewithal to retrieve it", they could still be prosecuted for possessing the image.

Representative Examples Schedule: This includes a table of example files. These include the name of the file, a description of the file and the location of it on the device, referred to as "the path or file path". It may also include an entry for the "MD5 Hash"; MD5 is an algorithm that can take any text or a file and create an ID like a fingerprint. The same file will always produce the same identifier. It allows you to verify that the file is unchanged or to compare two files to see if they are identical without actually opening the file. Hashing is important in evidence handling to assist in maintaining the chain of evidence and prevent tampering. We will discuss other types of hashing and file identification in Chapter 8.

Aggravating Factor(s): Where applicable, the forensic investigator may include the details of any aggravating factors they deem to present in the evidence. In the case of child sexual abuse material, this might include, for example, the age or vulnerability of the child, apparent distress or suffering, the period over which the images were possessed/distributed or produced, and any attempts to dispose or conceal the evidence. NB: *For those working in the treatment, assessment or risk management of offenders, this table of aggravating factors might be especially useful for you.*

If an alleged perpetrator does not volunteer the password to their device, the police have various tools that they can use to try and open the device without the password. One of these is GreyKey, often referenced in forensic reports.

One of the questions I am frequently asked by professionals working with online offenders is how likely it is that an offender simply found themselves inadvertently accessing child abuse material through clicking on a pop-up. Quite often, the offender will claim this is how they happened to be in possession of the indecent material. The answer is that this is very unlikely, but the file paths and the accessibility of the images could be a good indicator of this. Are they under a cache location for a web browser like Internet Explorer? It is possible that they did inadvertently access child abuse material if the file location contains the word "cache", and if the file creation times are in the same timeframe. However, if the file creation times are spread across a period, that would indicate multiple visits to the source of the abusive material. This information may or may not be contained within the forensic report as reports differ in their content.

Categorising indecent or extreme images

There have been two different methods of grading the severity of child abuse material proposed. The Sentencing Council Guidelines (Sentencing Council, 2013) identify five levels of images based on the COPINE (Combating Paedophile Information Networks in Europe) scale (Quayle, 2008):

- Level 1: images depicting erotic posing with no sexual activity
- Level 2: non-penetrative sexual activity between children or solo masturbation by a child

- Level 3: non-penetrative sexual activity between adults and children
- Level 4: penetrative sexual activity involving a child or children or both children and adults
- Level 5: sadism or penetration of, or by, an animal

The Council consulted with police and the CPS about the classification of images and in 2014 went on to propose a simplified three-level grading system which is currently in use in courts in England and Wales for crimes involving indecent images of children:

- Category A: images involve penetrative sexual activity, sexual activity with an animal or sadism.
- Category B: images involving non-penetrative sexual activity
- Category C: other indecent images not falling within categories A and B.

Psychological considerations: distorted/common beliefs or justifications for offenders

WHAT ARE COGNITIVE DISTORTIONS?

It is beyond the scope of this part of the chapter to explore the history of research around cognitive distortions, debates around their definition and the sometimes competing views of their relevance to offending and treatment (see Maruna & Mann, 2006, for a helpful review of the term and what it means for risk assessment and treatment). Abel and colleagues (1984) published seminal work on defining cognitive distortions as a form of cognitive adaptation in order to excuse ones offending behaviour, and the Sex Offender Treatment Programme (Beech et al., 1998) offered within His Majesty's Prison and Probation Service for many years included focus on exploring and challenging such beliefs. The term "cognitive distortion" can be used interchangeably with other terms, including offence supportive beliefs (Mann et al., 2007) and faulty schemas (Mann & Beech, 2003). Irrespective of the way they are defined, cognitive distortions can be a powerful perpetuating factor within someone's offending behaviour, because if distorted beliefs are relevant to ones offending they are often employed before, during, and after committing an offence (Szumski et al., 2018).

ARE THERE UNIQUE DISTORTIONS TO INTERNET OFFENDERS?

Howitt and Sheldon (2006) compared the cognitive distortions of contact and non-contact sexual offenders, and found that online sexual offenders had more distortions than contact sexual offenders on the subject of 'children are sexual beings', for example, the distorted belief that "*sometimes children don't say no to sexual activity with an adult because they are curious about sex or enjoy it*". However, the authors recognised some differences between online and contact sexual offenders, noting that the cognitive distortions which were most characteristic of online only sexual offenders were "*having sexual thoughts and fantasies about a child isn't all that bad because at least it is not really hurting the child*" and "*just looking at a naked child is not as bad as touching and will not affect the child as much*".

Over a decade later, Steel and colleagues (2020) conducted a systematic review and found that those who committed online sexual offences presented with a low level of endorsement of cognitive distortions traditionally associated with contact sex offenders, and the authors advocated for psychometric instruments which measure cognitive distortions that are specific to online sexual offenders, such as the Cognitions on Internet Sexual Offending (C-ISO) Scale (Paquette & Cortoni, 2019). Within their 2022 paper, Paquette and Cortoni describe the method through which they derived four themes which comprised the C-ISO:

— *Interpersonal relationship:* This category includes distortions around the world as an unsafe place (e.g. "*you cannot rely on anybody in life, you need to selfish*"), children as partners (e.g. "*I am at the same emotional level as children*") and entitlement (e.g. "*what I wanted was sexual intercourse with someone, so I looked for this within children with whom it's easier. I didn't care how old the person was*").
— *Sexualisation of children:* Distortions around the child as a sexual being (e.g. "*I knew she was underage, but I asked her if she was willing to sex chat with me before doing it*") and the nature of harm (e.g. "*At least I did not kidnap, kill or sexually abuse a child*").
— *Self:* Distortions around internal or external uncontrollability (e.g. "*the majority of the time, I was under the influence of alcohol when I sex chatted online with youths*", "*it was a rough period in my life, I had just divorced from my wife*", and "*I knew what I did was wrong, but it was more powerful than me*").
— *Internet:* Distortions around the Internet not being real (e.g. "*the images do not represent real sexual abuse*" and "*there's a different between role playing and real life*") and the Internet as an uncontrollable space (e.g. "*the images appeared as pop-ups on my computer without me wanting them*" and "*on the Internet, there is no barrier. Everything is too easily accessible*").

A more recent study by Bradbury and colleagues (2024) looked specifically at the distorted beliefs in those who engage in sexual conversations with children online, using the website Omegle (see Chapter 3 for information about Omegle and its closure). Bradbury and colleagues were interested in the reasons that adults might go online to seek out sexual conversations with minors on live chat apps and what strategies they might use to "neutralise" any feelings of guilt or shame about their behaviour. Themes derived include:

- *Denial and minimisation of responsibility:* Distortions around themselves having been manipulated, coerced, blaming the child and viewing themselves as a victim.
- *Child sexual abuse:* The individual is aware that they are conversing with a child, but suggests they were offered images/contact by the child.
- *Awareness of behaviour:* Beliefs around the platforms verified age requirement, loopholes around internal jurisdiction boundaries and the importance of there being a time lapse between the act and site action.

What we can draw from these studies, as examples of work in the area, is that while online sexual offenders may have different cognitive distortions to contact sexual offenders, they may not necessarily be any less frequent or any less potent; as with the study of psychology as a whole, we must consider the nuances of the individual in front of us and the salience of any distorted beliefs for them as a person.

HOW DO COGNITIVE DISTORTIONS PLAY A ROLE IN AN OFFENDER
GETTING CAUGHT?

While contact sexual offenders may more commonly offend alone (da Silva & Woodhams, 2019), the nature of the Internet and online offending behaviour means that there is an increased opportunity for offenders to come together, to discuss offending and to potentially share indecent imagery, for example. An offender with strong cognitive distortions minimising or justifying their behaviour may seek out like-minded individuals to reinforce these beliefs or to engage in co-offending, or they may develop cognitive distortions by virtue of interacting with others with offence-related beliefs online. There are various areas of the surface and dark web which can act as 'echo chambers' for harmful sexualised discussions. While that may seem a concerning thought, from a law enforcement perspective, these nefarious online social hubs offer an opportunity for catching those who are offending online, for example, through monitoring or undercover police work as described earlier in this chapter.

References

Abel, G. G., becker, J. V., & Cunningham-Rather, J. (1984). Complications, consent, and cognitions in sex between children and adults. *International Journal of Law and Psychiatry, 7*(1), 89–103.

Amnesty International UK. (2020, October 15). UK: MPs vote through 'deeply dangerous' Covert Human Intelligence Sources Bill. *Amnesty International UK*. Retrieved April 13, 2024, from https://www.amnesty.org.uk/press-releases/uk-mps-vote-through-deeply-dangerous-covert-human-intelligence-sources-bill

Bateson, R. (2021). The politics of vigilantism. *Comparative Political Studies, 54*, 923–955.

BBC News. (2019). Police concerns over rise of 'paedophile hunters'. Retrieved 7 July 2024 from https://www.bbc.co.uk/news/uk-england-50302912#:~:text=An%20assistant%20chief%20constable%20with,and%20often%20committed%20offences%20themselves

Beech, A. R. Fisher, D., & Becket, R. (1998). *Step 3: An evaluation of the prison Sex Offender Treatment Programme.* London: Home Office.

Bleakley, P. (2019, September 20). Watching the watchers: Taskforce Argos and the evidentiary issues involved with infiltrating Dark Web child exploitation networks. *The Police Journal, Theory, Practice and Principles, 92*(3), 221–236. https://journals.sagepub.com/doi/10.1177/0032258X18801409

Covert Human Intelligence Sources (Criminal Conduct) Act 2021. (2021). *Wikipedia.* Retrieved April 13, 2024, from https://www.legislation.gov.uk/ukpga/2021/4/section/1/enacted

Da Silva, T., & Woodhams, J. (2019). Introduction to the special issue on multiple perpetrator sexual offending. *Journal of Sexual Aggression, 25*(3), 323–225. https://doi.org/10.1080/13552600.2019.1681679

Drury, B., Drury, S. M., Rahman, A., & Ullah, I. (2022). A social network of crime: A review of the use of social networks for crime and the detection of crime. *Online Social Networks and Media, 30.* https://doi.org/10.1016/j.osnem.2022.100211

Europol. (2021, November 21). European Cybercrime Centre - EC3 | Europol. *Europol.* Retrieved April 13, 2024, from https://www.europol.europa.eu/about-europol/european-cybercrime-centre-ec3

Gross, G. (2020, March 13). Child exploitation bill earns strong opposition from encryption advocates. *Washington Examiner.* https://www.washingtonexaminer.com/policy/technology/2377798/child-exploitation-bill-earns-strong-opposition-from-encryption-advocates/

Kaye, D. (2017, June 1). Internal communication clearance form. *Internal Communication Clearance Form.* Retrieved August 3, 2024, from https://www.ohchr.org/sites/default/files/Documents/Issues/Opinion/Legislation/OL-DEU-1-2017.pdf

Lusthaus, J. (2018, September 19). Honour Among (Cyber)thieves? Honour Among (Cyber)thieves? https://ora.ox.ac.uk/objects/uuid:a19b4222-bd26-4b91-95aa-64c4e9d7adc6

Mann, R. E., & Beech, A. R. (2003). Cognitive distortions, schemas, and implicit theories. *Sexual Deviance: Issues and Controversies, 135*–153. https://doi.org/10.4135/9781483328751.n8

Mann, R. E., Webster, S., Wakeling, H., & Marshall, W. (2007). The measurement and influence of child sexual abuse supportive beliefs. *Psychology, Crime & Law: PC & L, 13*(5), 443–458.

Maruna, S., & Mann, R. E. (2006). A fundamental attribution error? Rethinking cognitive distortions. *Legal and Criminological Psychology, 11,* 155–177.

National Society for the Prevention of Cruelty to Children. (2023, August 15). 82% rise in online grooming crimes against children in the last 5 years. *NSPCC.* Retrieved April 21, 2024, from https://www.nspcc.org.uk/about-us/news-opinion/2023/2023-08-14-82-rise-in-online-grooming-crimes-against-children-in-the-last-5-years/

Newman, L. H. (2023, August 31). Apple's decision to kill its CSAM photo-scanning tool sparks fresh controversy. *WIRED.* Retrieved August 2, 2024, from https://www.wired.com/story/apple-csam-scanning-heat-initiative-letter/

Paquette, S., & Cortoni, F. (2019). The development and validation of the cognitions on internet sexual offending (C-ISO) scale. *Sexual Abuse, 32*(8), 907–930.

Paquette, S., & Cortoni, F. (2022). Offense-supportive cognitions expressed by men who use internet to sexually exploit children: A thematic analysis. *International Journal of Offender Therapy and Comparative Criminology, 66*(6–7), 647–669.

Porter, J. (2024, January 16). Google quietly updates Chrome's incognito warning in wake of tracking lawsuit. *The Verge*. Retrieved April 21, 2024, from https://www.theverge.com/2024/1/16/24039883/google-incognito-mode-tracking-lawsuit-notice-change

Quayle, E. (2008). The COPINE Project. *Irish Probation Journal, 5*, 65–83. Probation Boards for Northern Ireland.

Schoon, B., Li, A., Romero, A., & Wilde, D. (2022, August 22). Google locked parent's account over medical photos of their child; it's a good reminder to make backups. *9to5Google*. Retrieved August 2, 2024, from https://9to5google.com/2022/08/22/google-locked-account-medical-photo-story/

Senate Committee on the Judiciary. (2024, January 31). Big tech and the online child sexual exploitation crisis | United States Senate committee on the judiciary. *Senate Judiciary Committee*. Retrieved April 21, 2024, from https://www.judiciary.senate.gov/committee-activity/hearings/big-tech-and-the-online-child-sexual-exploitation-crisis

Sentencing Council. (2013). Sexual offences: Response to consultation. Retrieved 30 June, 2024 from https://www.sentencingcouncil.org.uk/wp-content/uploads/Final_Sexual_Offences_Response_to_Consultation_web1.pdf

Sentencing Council. (2017, February). *Imposition of community and custodial sentences*. Retrieved 30th June 2024 from https://www.sentencingcouncil.org.uk/overarching-guides/crown-court/item/imposition-of-community-and-custodial-sentences/

Steel, C. M. S., Newman, E., O'Rourke, S., & Quayle, E. (2020). A systematic review of cognitive distortions in online child sexual exploitation material offenders. *Aggression and Violent Behavior, 51*, 101375.

Sutherland V Her Majesty's Advocate. (2020). https://www.bailii.org/uk/cases/UKSC/2020/32.html

Szumski, F., Bartels, R. M., Beech, A. R., & Fisher, D. (2018). Distorted cognition related to male sexual offending: The multi-mechanism theory of cognitive distortions (MMT-CD). *Aggression and Violent Behavior, 39*, 139–151.

Tippett, A. (2022). The rise of paedophile hunters: To what extent are cyber-vigilante groups as productive form of policing, retribution and justice? *Criminology & Criminal Justice, 24*(4), 711–732.

U.S. Department of Homeland Security. (2022, January 10). Cyber crime cases. *Homeland security*. Retrieved April 13, 2024, from https://www.dhs.gov/cyber-crime-cases

Webber, A. (2020, May 13). Facebook to pay $52m for failing to protect staff from harmful content. *Personnel Today*. https://www.personneltoday.com/hr/facebook-moderators-settlement/

5 How online offenders evade detection

Christopher Wise and Jennifer Bamford

Introduction

This chapter is a crucial exploration of the tools, techniques and online services that online offenders employ to evade online detection. As mentioned in the Preface, this is not a how-to guide. However, it is essential to be aware that this information is readily available online and, unfortunately, widely used by online offenders. As those who offend online become more sophisticated, so do the efforts at apprehending them; someone who has evaded detection may not always do so. This chapter is designed to assist those involved in detection and/or risk management.

Encryption

As discussed in previous chapters, encryption has evolved from being reserved for processing online payments to becoming a standard for websites, email and messaging services. There are numerous types of encryption, and while exploring all of them is beyond the scope of this book, it is crucial to understand that the process of encryption generally involves the use of keys; these can take different forms, and the more complex the key, the stronger the encryption. Anyone with access to the key can decrypt and read the data; without it, it is unreadable.

The complexity of the algorithms and the size of keys used in the encryption have continued to increase over time. This has primarily been driven by the increase in the power of modern computers; as the processing power of computers increases, the amount of effort it takes to "brute force" the key is reduced. Brute force is the process of trial and error used to guess a code. By way of an example, an older encryption standard, Data Encryption Standard (DES), which was initially developed in the 1970s, was made obsolete in 2006 after the Universities of Bochum and Kiel broke DES encryption in nine days, using $10,000 worth of computer hardware. In 2008, they reduced this to one day (Kumar et al., 2009). Its replacement, the Advanced Encryption Standard (AES), has been approved for top-secret data by several government bodies, including the U.S. National Security Agency (Barker, 2006). While no encryption key is immune to compromise, it would take millions of years to brute force AES using present technologies.

DOI: 10.4324/9781003543794-5

End-to-end encryption

As we have discovered in the previous section, encryption has become ubiquitous with internet usage, and the algorithms in use today offer seemingly impossible-to-crack security and privacy. However, anyone with a key can use it to decrypt the data. In the case of websites, email services and messaging applications, the owners of those services have access to the keys and can use them to access their user's data. In general, this access is limited through the use of privacy policies. Still, in the event of a police investigation and subject to local legislation, the service provider will hand over the data to law enforcement and can decrypt the data to do so. End-to-end encryption (E2EE) differs from traditional encryption in that the service provider cannot access the keys; instead, the sender encrypts the data before being sent, and it is only possible for the intended recipient to decrypt and read the data. This form of encryption offers excellent security and is, in fact, a requirement for several regulatory frameworks, including the U.S. Health Insurance Portability and Accountability Act of 1996 (HIPAA; Alder, 2023).

Where E2EE has come under criticism is the limited access it provides law enforcement. When investigating crimes such as child exploitation, terrorism or drug trafficking, lawful interception of communications is often vital. Where E2EE is in use, law enforcement must gain access to a device that is part of the chain of communication to view the messages. Following the rise of E2EE, the UK government sought to introduce new legislation forcing service providers to create backdoor access, effectively breaking E2EE. This received significant backlash from privacy experts (Hern, 2016) and ultimately resulted in that legislation being removed from the Investigatory Powers Act 2016.

E2EE is widespread across messaging services, including all Meta-owned platforms – WhatsApp, Messenger and Instagram. However, it has yet to be widely used across the most commonly used email platforms, such as Gmail. Several new privacy-focused email platforms have started to gain popularity and feature E2EE as one of several additional security controls they offer as part of their service.

The debate around the use of E2EE is still ongoing. As of writing, no current legislation exists ruling that it should be banned or that service providers must create a backdoor for government agencies to intercept these encrypted communications, which results in evident difficulties when it comes to apprehending individuals using these platforms to facilitate crime.

Virtual private networks

To briefly recap Chapter 1, we discussed the nuts and bolts of the Internet, including the role of Internet service providers and protocols. In particular, we discussed how Internet Protocol (IP) addresses are one of the unique digital fingerprints used to identify the premises where someone has accessed a website or application. We also covered what information is available to Internet service providers and how they can retain and share it with law enforcement.

Virtual private networks, almost always referred to as VPNs, have become more commonplace. Initially, VPNs were exclusively used by large corporations to provide access to internal networks between locations and for remote employees, and they are still regularly used for this purpose. Consumer-focused VPN services have emerged following increased awareness of online privacy and security concerns. According to a recent survey by Forbes, 76% of the British public is aware of VPNs, and of those surveyed, 42% use a VPN for personal or business reasons (Hooson, 2024).

VPNs provide additional security by providing a private-encrypted digital "tunnel." A user connects to the Internet as they would normally. Once connected, they can enable the VPN software. Once enabled, this software will connect the person's device to the VPN provider's network through a specialised tunnel, another form of protocol (see Chapter 1 for a description of protocols). What makes this particular protocol special is the layers of encryption that hide the content of the data travelling through it from anyone watching the network, including any devices on the same network, Internet service providers and law enforcement. Once arriving at the VPN provider network, the web traffic leaves the tunnel and enters the Internet normally. However, the IP address is that of the VPN providers, not the IP address of the originating user. Only the VPN provider knows that information. The most popular and secure VPN providers are considered "no-log". This means that they do not keep any records of their customers' internet use. Even if law enforcement obtains access to the VPN provider's data through a warrant, there would not be any data of value to an investigation.

Not all VPNs are created equal; only a tiny number are independently audited to demonstrate that they do not keep logs, or in the case of ExpressVPN, through the seizure of their servers. In 2017, following the 2016 assassination of Russia's ambassador to Turkey, Andrei Korlov, Turkish authorities seized the servers of ExpressVPN looking for logs of conversations related to the crime but turned up nothing (Crawford, 2017). Using a VPN can also make it appear that a user is accessing the Internet from a different country, further hindering law enforcement efforts and causing jurisdictional issues.

Anonymised communication platforms

As we have covered, the rise of E2EE is a complicated topic, with both privacy advocates and governments arguing the benefits versus the dangers. Regardless of the outcome of those debates and any laws enacted. It is highly likely that anonymised communication platforms will always be available to people who offend online, and as some are banned or taken down by law enforcement, newer, more sophisticated alternatives will take their place. A well-known anonymised platform was Encrochat, which provided modified smartphones with specialised privacy features, such as encryption, chat service and a "kill pill" (a password that, when used, would automatically wipe the device clean to destroy any evidence of the owner's activities). Encrochat was famously taken down by law enforcement after confiscating its servers, which resulted in numerous arrests across multiple countries (Stedman, 2023). While no alternative has yet to fill the void, criminals actively use mainstream platforms due to the security and privacy they now promise.

With Meta's purchase of WhatsApp, a general sense of mistrust emerged in user data privacy. Despite the claims of E2EE, many law-abiding users began to look at alternative options. The two most popular alternatives are Signal and Telegram. Telegram, in particular, has become a popular option for online offenders because it has a group feature, unlike its pure messaging app equivalents. This group feature has allowed drug dealers and distributors of child abuse material the ability to advertise what they have for sale anonymously. Research conducted by the Finnish-based child rights NSO Protect Children found that Telegram was the most popular messaging app used to "search for, view, and share CSAM"[1] (Suojellaan Lapsia, Protect Children ry, 2024).

The dark web – a deeper dive

The dark web might be considered the shadowy corner of the Internet. If we reflect on our iceberg view of the Internet as described in Chapter 1, even if it represents a minuscule part of the Web, it is a small part of something unimaginably massive. There is more than one dark web. However, the one that most people refer to when talking about the dark web is The Onion Relay (TOR) network. It was released in 2002, but its origins go back to the 1990s when the U.S. Naval Research Lab researched how to create an anonymous, secure communication method for U.S. intelligence communications. To this day, the non-profit organisation that maintains and improves the TOR project is partly funded by several U.S. federal agencies. Let us explore some key things that set the dark web apart from the regular Internet.

Designed and built to create anonymity

Thinking back to the post office analogy in Chapter 1, what allowed our ISPs and law enforcement to track the websites visited by web users was the IP address and how it is visible to anyone handling our data as it moves from our devices to the Internet, and ultimately to its destination. In the case of the dark web, you can imagine it as passing through a maze-like network of encrypted servers called relays; there are three hops through this maze, and anyone monitoring the Internet will see requests coming from the last relay in this maze referred to as the exit relay, not from a person's device. As we have discussed, someone's IP address is the digital fingerprint used by law enforcement to identify their web activity. In the case of the dark web, only the exit relay IP address is visible, which makes it nearly impossible to determine who or where the information was accessed or sent from.

Why is such a network not blocked by governments or law enforcement? The TOR network is banned in several countries, predominantly in authoritarian regimes such as China and Iran. However, the motivation for these bans is not concerned with illicit uses but positive ones (McCarthy, 2017). One of the main drivers for the TOR network is to provide a means for individuals in oppressive regimes to access the Internet and blocked sites and for journalists to share information. Even in countries where the TOR network is banned and actively blocked, volunteers worldwide provide a way to bypass this. Known as TOR bridges, they provide a secret way of accessing the TOR network.

It cannot be indexed or crawled

Search engines such as Google, Yahoo and Bing use indexing to find and catalogue websites so that they can be found by website name or related keywords. Dark web search engines cannot apply this same indexing process to the TOR network as they use onion addresses; unlike their clear and deep web counterparts, they do not contain meaningful, human-readable words. Instead, they are made of 56 seemingly random numbers and letters. While dark web search engines exist, the sites listed within them have been registered by the owners of the websites. This means that should cyber criminals wish to act under the radar of law enforcement, they can operate dark web sites and only share the onion address with those they trust. Assuming that they are careful about whom they share these addresses with, they can remain completely undetected by law enforcement.

An overlay network built on top of the web

Without the Internet as we know it, the dark web's current form would not be possible. In the same way that the Internet was initially built on top of the telephone network, the dark web is built on or overlayed on the Internet. This means that to access the dark web, a person will always need to have a connection to the Internet.

It is impossible to access "accidentally"

Accessing the dark web or TOR network requires specialised software. Due to the added encryption and complex routes, any data being sent or received requires a dedicated application like the TOR browser to be installed. However, at the time of writing, one Internet browser offers it similarly to "Incognito" mode. It does not provide the same level of security and anonymity as the TOR browser, but it does make accessing the dark web even easier.

Cryptocurrencies

The emergence of cryptocurrencies has ushered in a new era for online offenders, providing them with a financial system built with anonymity at its core. These digital currencies, designed with principles of decentralisation and pseudonymity, quickly became the preferred transaction method for anyone seeking to sidestep traditional financial surveillance. While cryptocurrencies offer legitimate uses, online offenders have exploited their inherent privacy features to move illicit funds and obscure their identities.

Unlike traditional banking systems, where transactions are tied to real-world identities, cryptocurrencies use pseudonymous addresses, making it difficult to link transactions to individuals directly. This feature of cryptocurrencies allows online offenders to act with a level of anonymity previously unattainable using traditional banking methods. The decentralised nature of cryptocurrencies further complicates efforts to track and trace illicit funds.

Online offenders can effortlessly transfer funds across international borders without the scrutiny and delays associated with traditional financial institutions. This ability to move funds quickly and anonymously has made cryptocurrencies the payment method of choice for ransomware attacks, dark web marketplaces and other illicit activities.

While cryptocurrencies offer a significant degree of privacy, the belief that cryptocurrencies offer *complete* anonymity is a misconception. Despite creating additional challenges for law enforcement, the development of specialist analysis tools and the increasing cooperation between authorities and cryptocurrency exchanges, it is becoming increasingly difficult for criminals to operate undetected. Cryptocurrency exchanges are platforms used to exchange cryptocurrencies for other currencies, both digital and regular. The nature of cryptocurrency technology, known as blockchain, means that every transaction is recorded and potentially traceable, providing a valuable resource for law enforcement agencies.

Cryptocurrencies have shifted the balance of power in the ongoing cat-and-mouse game between law enforcement and online offenders. However, as technology evolves and new investigative techniques emerge, criminals' ability to exploit cryptocurrencies' anonymity may decline.

External risk management for online sexual offenders

For those working in risk management, i.e. probation officers, you will already be familiar with the various conditions that can be implemented for those convicted of online sexual offences. These might be licence conditions if released from prison, or they might be conditions associated with someone's Sex Offender Registration (SOR) or a Sexual Harm Prevention Order (SHPO). These conditions might include, but are not limited to:

- Restricting someone's access to the Internet;
- Monitoring someone's use of internet-enabled devices;
- Prohibiting someone's access to certain applications or software, e.g. VPNs
- Prohibiting someone's access to social media and/or dating websites

For those who have committed online sexual offences only (i.e. no contact offending), the more 'traditional' licence conditions for those who have committed sexual offences may not be sufficient enough to manage risk. For example, monitoring someone's location using Global Positioning System (GPS) tagging and regular sign-ins at an Approved Premise is not likely to be relevant to those who have offended sexually online. However, it is also important to consider the risk of 'crossover' offending; that is, those individuals who have committed contact sexual offences may go on to commit online sexual offences and vice versa. It is an important balancing exercise in risk management, considering the ways in which risk could change or escalate in the future while being mindful of the individual's right to various freedoms.

While not all individuals go on to reoffend following apprehension, some do, and as we have deduced within this chapter already, sometimes those who offend online can be creative in trying to evade detection. It may therefore be helpful for those involved in risk management to be aware of the various practical or physical ways that online offenders can access or store illegal content, as described below.

Storage devices

When we think about online offences, we picture someone on their phone, laptop or PC. When caught, those devices are confiscated for forensic examination, and necessary evidence is captured and catalogued before finally being presented during a trial. However, as technology has become smaller and more accessible, including making its way into almost any home appliance you can think of, the myriad of options available to online offenders makes it a daunting task for police and law enforcement agencies. Within this section, we will explore some of the more unusual options available to online offenders to hide their online behaviour through alternative forms of technology and storage.

Remote or cloud servers

Once reserved for IT experts with professional experience in setting up and running these types of computers, the rise of cloud computing has made it extremely easy for anyone able to follow online instructions or even ask a service like Chat-GPT to provide detailed step-by-step guidance on how you would set up one of these machines in a well-known cloud provider such as Google or Amazon. With cloud-hosted servers, there is no physical machine in an online offenders' home. Instead, they can run remote servers in a data centre anywhere in the world, remotely accessing them using the dark web, a VPN or even both. While these cloud providers have terms and conditions prohibiting the use of their services for criminal conduct, using the anonymity-providing tools we have discussed in this chapter would make it challenging for the cloud provider to spot this misuse.

These remote machines can operate in the same way any home computer can, but, when accessed remotely, leave no trace on the home computer being used to access it. If the police raid an online offenders' home, unless it is very quickly identified that a remote server was being used to evade detection, the offender could quickly destroy the remote machine before the police forensic experts discover that one was being used.

Removable storage

We have all seen and used portable USB disks for backups and transferring files to colleagues and friends. However, most people may not know that it is possible to plug a USB drive into a PC or laptop and start up a completely independent operating system and file system. While the host PC is powered on, and its peripherals and processing power are being used, its hard drive is not. Any files downloaded and the history of websites accessed will be stored on the USB drive, or in some cases, not at all. This type of USB stick computer may seem highly specialised and require substantial technical knowledge to set up and run. However, the most significant trend with technology in recent years is how accessible and consumer-friendly it has become. There is a privacy-focused operating system built specifically for this way of working whereby nothing the users do is recorded, and every time it is started, it is a clean slate. No actions performed by the user or files downloaded persist after it is restarted, nor will any forensic evidence be retrievable from either the computer it is connected to or the USB disk itself.

Removable storage can take many forms, from USB sticks and removable hard drives to network-based storage that doesn't need a connection to a computer to be accessed. Storage technology has progressed dramatically over the last three decades; at one time, the cost of a one-gigabyte drive was the same as a laptop today, despite having only a fraction of the storage of a modern smartphone. It has also become much smaller, with the most miniature storage cards no larger than the nail on your little finger. USB storage has also started taking many forms and disguised as everyday objects. The ability for these ever-shrinking USB drives to be hidden in plain sight and take on almost any disguise imaginable presents a challenge for law enforcement and professionals working with people who offend online. In one such example shared with me, the police had raided the home of a suspected online offender, and the accused had his phone and laptop taken as evidence. The accused pointed out their collection of servers to police officers, each fully capable of accessing the Internet and storing masses of data. However, the police chose not to take them, quite possibly not recognising the servers for what they were.

Psychological considerations: Risk management in therapy/within client assessments for those who have sexually offended online

Anecdotally, a common area of debate amongst clinicians (therapists and psychologists) is around balancing someone's freedom with risk management. Can we realistically prevent someone from accessing the Internet if they have committed online offences? Is this even fair/justifiable in an increasingly digital world? Another associated consideration might be how someone with a history of sexual offending can realistically and safely meet their sexual needs, and hence, consideration should be given as to the individual's plans regarding whether or not they will use online pornography, for example, to meet their sexual needs. For many who have felt their online behaviour has been an addiction, complete abstinence may be the most appropriate solution. For others, there may be a middle ground somewhere.

From the author's experience of assessing a number of online offenders and speaking to various therapists working in the field, there have been some useful creative solutions for risk management shared when it comes to accessing pornography, which may be helpfully listed here:

- To only access pornographic DVDs or magazines (to avoid online pornography which is less controllable).
- To set up an 'accountability partner' who will receive emails every time you access pornography, as a form of tracking. There are online services providing this.
- To have a 'pornography plan' which includes a set time limit that pornography will be accessed for, a specific legal website to be accessed, and for safe and healthy search terms to be agreed in therapy.

Similarly, discussing a plan around broader access to internet-enabled devices may be appropriate for your client. For example, ensuring that any device they have access to is only used in high-traffic areas, sharing the device password with someone close to them who also has access, and having a plan around times of day to access the Internet. For those whose sexual behaviour has become a preoccupation or 'addiction' a referral to support services, such as Sex Addicts Anonymous, may also be of assistance.

While external risk management is likely to be important when working with someone with a history of online sexual offending, in therapy or assessment, we might often explore with a client their understanding of how they can manage their own risk to assess their level of self-awareness. Formulating a collaborative risk management plan can be a useful part of this process wherein the client considers a range of warning signs of increasing risk and strategies to manage these. This might be a piece of work that is reviewed and amended over time as their lifestyle changes or there is a change in their understanding around their risk and triggers.

Note

1 CSAM: Child Sexual Abuse Material.

References

Alder, S. (2023, April 11). *How to make your Email HIPAA Compliant*. The HIPAA Journal. Retrieved June 1, 2024, from https://www.hipaajournal.com/make-your-email-hipaa-compliant/

Barker, E. (2006, March 22). *Suite B Cryptography*. NIST Computer Security Resource Center. Retrieved June 1, 2024, from https://csrc.nist.gov/CSRC/media/Events/ISPAB-MARCH-2006-MEETING/documents/E_Barker-March2006-ISPAB.pdf

Crawford, D. (2017, December 20). *ExpressVPN Cannot Hand over Logs to Turkish Police because It Has None*. ProPrivacy.com. Retrieved May 4, 2024, from https://proprivacy.com/privacy-news/expressvpn-cannot-hand-over-logs

Hern, A. (2016, January 12). *Privacy Watchdog Attacks Snooper's Charter Over Encryption*. The Guardian. https://www.theguardian.com/technology/2016/jan/12/privacy-watchdog-attacks-snoopers-charter-encryption

Hooson, M. (2024, April 30). *VPN Statistics and Trends – Forbes Advisor UK*. Forbes. Retrieved May 4, 2024, from https://www.forbes.com/uk/advisor/business/vpn-statistics/

Kumar, S., Paar, C., Pelzl, J., Pfeiffer, G., Rupp, A., & Schimmler, M. (2009). How to Break DES for BC, 8,980. https://www.researchgate.net/publication/228937703_How_to_Break_DES_for_BC_8980

McArdle, B. (2021, April 28). *How Hackers Use Cloud Services to Make Cybercrime More Profitable*. Infosecurity Magazine. Retrieved May 21, 2024, from https://www.infosecurity-magazine.com/blogs/how-hackers-use-cloud-services/

McCarthy, K. (2017, July 11). *Russia, China Vow to Kill Off VPNs, Tor Browser*. The Register. https://www.theregister.com/2017/07/11/russia_china_vpns_tor_browser/

Stedman, H. (2023, October 9). *Crime 'Kingpins' among 400 Jailed after Police Crack 'Secure' Chat App*. The Independent. https://www.independent.co.uk/news/uk/home-news/met-police-encrochat-b2426469.html

Suojellaan Lapsia, Protect Children ry. (2024, February 20). *Tech Platforms Used by Online Child Sexual Abuse Offenders*. https://www.suojellaanlapsia.fi/. Retrieved May 6, 2024, from https://bd9606b6-40f8-4128-b03a-9282bdcfff0f.usrfiles.com/ugd/bd9606_0d8ae7365a8f4bfc977d8e7aeb2a1e1a.pdf

6 Online sexual offending and the law

Nicholas Wragg and Angus McWilliams

Introduction

The legal landscape of online sexual offences in England and Wales is a complex and evolving domain. Never has it been so important; child abuse imagery proliferates online and no social media space feels safe from predators. The legal framework is being stretched and tested by advancing technology. An era of artificial intelligence (AI) presents a new world of challenge but may also bring hope of technology-based solutions, as discussed elsewhere in this book.

This chapter provides an overview of the current legal framework. The first part of this chapter addresses the different commonly encountered online sexual offences, categorising them primarily into image-based and communication-based offences; these distinctions often overlap. The second part of this chapter considers the investigation and prosecution of such offences, to help understand how offending behaviour can be detected and brought to justice. The chapter also explores the evolving approach of the criminal justice system in recognising the seriousness of these offences, and in particular how courts have given ever-increasing weight to intended harm, not only actual harm.

Much of the law relating to illegal sexual imagery and sexual communication is not new, but has proved remarkably robust in the face of evolving technologies, surviving essentially unchanged through the explosion of home Internet in the late 1990s and the arrival of high-speed broadband in the early 2000s. Likewise, the law itself has proved sufficiently versatile to largely cope with the revolution that is social media, even if the lives of children and young adults in particular may never be the same again. AI and the proliferation of deepfake material is severely testing these long-drafted provisions, but it is rarely loopholes in the law that allow such harmful content to be a painfully common aspect of online life. Enforcement and Regulation has been given a welcome new emphasis by the Online Safety Act 2023 (see Chapter 4 for more details on the Act), but in the meantime, the relevant internet safety teams of police forces across England and Wales remain stretched to their limits.

At the heart of the criminal law in this field are victims, often children, from all over the planet. The protection of children and victims of sexual offending is central to all that is done in the criminal justice system in this arena, and the fact

DOI: 10.4324/9781003543794-6

that harmful and offending behaviours increasingly arise through the medium of the Internet is irrelevant. Their voices may not be heard loudly enough or often enough, but if the Internet can foster a sense of unreality for some, it does not for the victims of abuse the world over. The incredible world of opportunity that exists online, and which entwines all of our lives, has a miserably dark aspect. The law must and does break any veneer of harmlessness. Understanding the applicable law and legal processes is to understand that effective enforcement has never been more important. Reducing harm and risk is a challenge for all of society and the law must play its part.

Online offences

There are a myriad of online sexual offences, which, for the purpose of this chapter, are broken down into image offending and communication offending. These offences are primarily contained in the Sexual Offences Act 2003, Protection of Children Act 1978, and Criminal Justice Act 1988. The law has always evolved to meet new demands, and this evolution continues.

An example of the law evolving to deal with technological change can be seen in the Protection of Children Act 1978. When originally enacted, Section 1(a) provided that it was an offence to take, or permit to be taken, any indecent photograph of a child (meaning in this Act a person under the age of 16). The current expression of Section 1(a) is to take, or permit to be taken or to make, any indecent photograph or pseudo-photograph of a child. These amendments are a result of the Criminal Justice and Public Order Act 1994, taking into account the development of the Internet as opposed to printed photographs. In addition, despite the age of consent remaining at 16, the relevant age in respect of sexual images was raised to 18. The current expression of the section refers to images of a child. A child is elsewhere defined as a person under the age of 18 (Children Act, 1989 s.105). The addition of pseudo-photographs in 1994 also takes into account technological developments in software which enable offending persons to edit images. This amendment presaged recent developments in AI which offending persons can use to create photorealistic indecent images of children (see Chapter 2 for more information about AI-generated imagery). The Online Safety Act 2023 represents a further step forward, especially in relation to sharing images online.

Indecent images of children

Indecent images are photographs or photorealistic images of children under the age of 18. There are three categories of indecent images: Categories A, B and C. Category A images depict children involved in penetrative sexual activity or involving sexual activity with an animal or sadism. Category B images depict children involved in non-penetrative sexual activity. Category C images are all other indecent images of children not falling in Category A or B (Sentencing Council, 2014).

Prohibited images of children are cartoon or anime-style images depicting child sexual abuse material of an obscene character (Coroners and Justice Act,

2009 s62). Unlike indecent images, prohibited images can only be charged if the individual is in possession of the images (see 'Making' below).

There are several components to indecent images of children offences. Firstly, the still or moving image must be a photograph or pseudo-photograph. The Protection of Children Act 1978 as amended defines 'photograph' widely, to include data stored on a computer or disc that is capable of conversion to a photograph, negatives of photographs, a tracing or a film. The second component is that the 'photograph' must be 'indecent' in nature. This is an objective test and can take into account the age of the child depicted (R v Neal, 2011). The motivation of the individual taking the photograph is irrelevant (R v Graham-Kerr, 1989). The final component is that the image is of a child, an individual under the age of 18 (Protection of Children Act 1978 s7). In cases where there is no direct evidence of the age of the person depicted (which is the vast majority of cases involving online offenders), this is a matter for the finders of fact, i.e the jury in a Crown Court, the District Judge or Magistrates in a Magistrates' Court. Expert evidence is not admissible (R v Land, 1998). As a matter of course, investigating police officers with appropriate training will provide estimates of the age of the child depicted along with brief written descriptions of imagery, to assist the court and practitioners in dealing with these cases without themselves viewing the material.

There are four indecent images of children offences related to Making, Possession, Distribution and Taking (Protection of Children Act, 1978 s1):

- *Making* is interpreted as the doing of a deliberate act with the knowledge that it is likely to result in an indecent image appearing on a device. This can include downloading an indecent image (R v Jayson, 2003) or receiving an image from someone, for example, on social media or email. Images come from a wide variety of sources including online chat forums, file image hosting sites and via the dark web.
- *Possession* relates to saved or stored images where an individual has such images in his control (R v Okoro, 2018) and the individual is capable of accessing the images without the use of specialist software.
- *Distribution* takes place where a person parts possession of an image or exposes or offers it for acquisition by another person. The most obvious forms of distribution include cases where people send others such images regardless of whether they are physical, i.e. photographs or digital versions. Those who send links to such images are also caught by this provision, as are those who use peer-to-peer or torrent sites that permit the downloading and dissemination of such images. Section 1(1)(c) of the Protection of Children Act, 1978, is a seldom used provision which criminalises those who have images in their possession with a view to it being distributed or shown by the perpetrator to others.
- *Taking*, or producing, indecent images (Protection of Children Act, 1978 s1) refers to an individual deliberately and intentionally manufacturing an indecent image (R v D.M, 2011). This includes the physical taking of images on a camera or the creation of a unique image by editing pre-existing images of children (i.e. a pseudo image). Those who use AI software to create such images will be liable

to be charged with producing an indecent image or pseudo image. In 2023, the Internet Watch Foundation came across the first reports of indecent images being created by AI. In a one-month period, 2,562 AI-generated indecent images were posted to a single dark web forum (Internet Watch Foundation, 2023).

Extreme pornographic images

Extreme Pornographic Images are images that portray pornographic and grossly offensive material that depicts in a realistic way acts including but are not limited to; bestiality, necrophilia or rape (Criminal Justice and Immigration Act, 2008, p. 5). Such imagery is routinely encountered by law enforcement during investigations of online offending. The harm involved in the production of such material can itself be profound. Additionally, the proliferation of this material itself causes significant harm. This may be to victims portrayed in the imagery itself. Furthermore, the relatively easy availability of such material online, especially to children, is a matter of considerable and increasing concern. The illegality of such material may not be as widely understood.

'Pornographic' material is of such a nature that it must reasonably be assumed to have been produced solely or principally for the purposes of sexual arousal. Such an image will be extreme if it portrays in an explicit and realistic way various prohibited extreme acts. The material must also be grossly offensive, disgusting or otherwise obscene. As with indecent images of children, an image may be still or moving and also includes data stored by any means that is capable of conversion into an image.

Sharing intimate images

A person commits an offence if they intentionally share or threaten to share an image which shows another person in an intimate state, when the other does not consent and when the person does not reasonably believe the other consented. This offence is commonly known as 'revenge pornography'. The purpose of the person committing this offence might, in addition to simply doing the act, be to cause alarm, distress or humiliation or to obtain sexual gratification for themselves or another. This sharing need not necessarily be online, but invariably will be. This area of law was considerably strengthened by the Online Safety Act (2023). This offence applies equally to indecent images of children as to adult pornography. If the images shared portray a child in an intimate state, then it may also be illegal as an indecent image of a child.

Cyber flashing

An offence relating to the sending or sharing of pictures of genitals is committed when an individual sends a photograph or film of any person's genitals to another person intending to cause them alarm, distress or humiliation or does so for the purpose of obtaining sexual gratification and is reckless as to whether they cause them alarm, distress or humiliation (Sexual Offences Act, 2003 s66). A 'photograph' might be of a real person but also includes computer-generated imagery which appears to be a photograph. The photograph might be of the sender's own genitals or might come from any other source. This could include a photograph of the recipient's own genitals.

The offence does require the sender to either intend or at least be reckless about whether their actions will cause alarm, distress or humiliation. This may mean that consensual sharing of images of genitals, for example between consenting adults, is less likely to amount to an offence. It may also mean that the sharing of otherwise legal pornographic images will not likely amount to an offence.

However, the offence is widely drafted. While the headline has been to tackle the scourge of so-called 'cyber flashing' – sending unsolicited a picture of one's genitals to another – the sharing of any image of any person's genitals is caught, presuming there is the requisite intent. This could include sharing many otherwise lawful pornographic images, for example, especially if the sender intended or was reckless about causing distress for personal, religious or cultural reasons. Furthermore, although the offence will often arise by sending an image online, for example on a social media platform or phone app, it is also committed by showing the other person such an image or by placing it for a particular person to find (such as into an online storage facility).

Deepfakes

Deepfake images have been digitally manipulated to replace one person's likeness with that of another. Creating fake content is not new, but readily available tools and techniques, including those leveraging AI, have made this a more urgent topic. While much online deepfaking was once targeted at celebrities, the creation and sharing of deepfake sexual imagery online has rapidly become commonplace (see Chapter 2 for further information on deepfakes and the technology behind them).

In many instances, the existing legal framework will be sufficient to capture such behaviour when it is harmful. Deepfake indecent images that portray children will likely involve the production of illegal images. Manipulating existing pornographic images to portray a known person and then sharing it online is likely to be an offence as described above.

However, this is an area where legal gaps may exist. In the UK, since at least the early 2020s, some have proposed banning the very creation of a sexually explicit deepfake image without the consent of those involved, with more severe penalties for those who share such material. Far from being a problem only for celebrities, the widespread availability of cheap or free apps that allow the production of such material in seconds means the problem is one that merits further legal development. It is a problem across multiple arenas as deepfake imagery proliferates, perhaps especially in politics, sport, celebrity life and anyone for whom reputation matters (see Chapter 2 for more details about deepfakes and sextortion).

Communication offences

The Sexual Offences Act 2003 sets out a number of sexual offences that can be committed online. These offences do not exist only online by any means, but online behaviours are where very many such offences manifest. Included here are a combination of specific communication offences and offences which commonly arise in online communication cases.

Sexual communication with a child

A person over 18 years of age commits an offence of sexual communication with a child (Sexual Offences Act, 2003 s15) if, for the purpose of sexual gratification, they intentionally communicate with a person under 16 (and who they do not reasonably believe to be over 16) and the communication is sexual. The tests for determining whether an individual has a reasonable belief, or whether the communications are sexualised, are objective.

Cause/incite a child to engage in sexual activity

This offence requires a person, over the age of 18, to intentionally cause or incite (encourage) a child under the age of 16 to engage in a sexual activity, not reasonably believing the child is over 16 (Sexual Offences Act, 2003 s10). A separate and more serious offence is committed where the child is under 13 (Sexual Offences Act, 2003 s8).

The difference between 'causing' and 'inciting' relates to whether the alleged sexual activity has taken place. If an individual 'causes' a child to engage in sexual activity, it directly implies that the activity took place. 'Inciting' relates to persuading or encouraging even if the intended activity does not occur. 'Sexual activity' encompasses a wide variety of behaviours including physical acts such as touching or undressing but can also include encouraging or inciting a child to take an indecent photograph of themselves or communicate sexually.

Cause a child to view a sexual act

This offence is committed where a person over the age of 18 intentionally causes a child under the age of 16 to watch a sexual act for the purposes of obtaining sexual gratification themselves and that the individual does not reasonably believe the person they are speaking to is over 16 (Sexual offences Act, 2003 s12). The sexual act that a child can view includes a live or recorded sexual act and may be a moving or still image.

Arrange/facilitate a child sexual offence

A person commits an offence if they intentionally arrange or facilitate something that they intend to do, intend another person to do or believes that another person will do, and doing so will involve the commission of an offence under sections 5–13 of the Sexual Offences Act 2003. The terms 'arrange' and 'facilitate' are not defined within the Sexual Offences Act, and the courts will take a wide but dictionary interpretation. To arrange means to plan something in advance, whereas facilitating something involves assisting or making it easier.

An example of 'arranging' within the context of this offence could be where an individual makes a plan with an adult to meet a child for the purposes of sexual activity. An example of 'facilitating' might be where another individual knowingly drives a person to the meeting, regardless of whether they intended to engage in such activity themselves. These offences will be considered to be 'complete' when the arrangements for the intended offence are made or the intended offence has been facilitated. It is not a requirement that the offence takes place or that it is possible (R v Privett and Others, 2020). There are exceptions and defence for those properly supporting children, for example with contraception or healthcare.

This offence arises commonly in online law enforcement, typically through chatroom and social media communications. The communications might be between adult and child or between adult and adult, about a child. Communications often begin on mainstream, lawful online spaces and then move to one-to-one messaging apps. Such interactions might last minutes, or might range over days, weeks or months, and often multiple offences arise during the course of these communications. This offending will almost invariably result in a prison sentence. It is important to recognise that the underlying intention of a person committing this offence is that there will be a real child sexual offence taking place.

Meeting a child following sexual grooming

A person commits an offence if they intentionally communicate with a person, under 16, on one or more occasions and subsequently travels to meet them with the intention of committing a relevant offence at the time of the meeting or on some later occasion (Sexual offences Act, 2003 s15). This offence can be committed where no meeting takes place, as soon as a person sets off on their journey. In cases involving undercover police officers or vigilante stings, an offending person is typically confronted at the point of their planned meeting. However, the law is designed to allow law enforcement not to wait. A relevant offence is an offence under Part 1 of the Sexual Offences Act 2003 and includes but is not limited to rape, sexual assault and causing a child to engage in sexual activity (Sexual Offences Act, 2003). The communication prior to travel does not need to be sexual; it is enough to prove an intention to commit an offence when they meet the child.

This offence is erroneously referred to as an offence of 'grooming'. There is no specific offence of 'grooming', although the communications may, depending on the words or behaviour used, be captured by other communication offences. Grooming-type behaviours often arise in online cases; these may include pretending to be someone else or of a different age, offering advice or understanding, buying gifts, giving attention, using a professional position or reputation and offering trips or outings or other opportunities. There is no closed list, but such grooming behaviours are likely to aggravate any offence arising and be relevant to risk management.

Decoy and so-called 'victimless' cases

It is often the case that law enforcement encounters a person committing such online communication offences, but it is not possible to be sure that there is a real child victim. This might be because it is known that the other person operating a so-called 'decoy' was an undercover police officer or civilian vigilante. It might be because evidence of the communication has been recovered online or from a device, but the other person, often purporting to be a child, cannot be traced or identified as a child. Law enforcement dedicates significant resources to victim tracing, but it may often be impossible or impracticable. These cases are distinct from where it is known that the other participant was a child, but their identity remains unknown.

In all of these communication offences, it is the belief and intention of the person committing the offence that is crucial. If the offending person believes they are speaking to or about a real child, they will be guilty. The fact that there was no real child, or that it cannot be determined whether there was a real child or not is generally irrelevant to whether an offence has been committed.

Many such instances will be prosecuted as an 'attempted' offence on the basis that the person committing the offence attempted to do it, but unbeknownst to them there was no real child. In arranging or facilitating offences, it is never necessary to use the word 'attempt', because the person committing the offence is making the arrangements for what they believe will be a real offence come what may, even if it would never have been possible. Assessing the seriousness of such decoy cases is discussed further below.

Obscene and offensive publications

There are a wide range of communication offences which may arise in respect of online sexual offending. The sending of grossly offensive, indecent or obscene messages, indecent displays and encouraging or assisting an offence are all captured in different areas of law when the particular circumstances arise. 'Obscene' publications are those that tend to depravity or corruption. This goes beyond the ordinary meaning of obscene but will often cover online communications regarding child abuse. The courts have interpreted 'publications' to include otherwise entirely private communications between two people online, even when they are using encrypted, secure channels. This form of offence typically arises when two adults discuss the commission of child abuse or how they would like to engage in child abuse. The offence here does not necessarily involve an intent to actually commit such an offence on a child but may arise in the sharing of child abuse stories or the exchange of fantasy messaging regarding child abuse.

The role of online platforms and services

In 2023, the Online Safety Act 2023 received Royal assent and became law. The Act introduces measures in an attempt to combat online harm to both children and adults. It places significantly more responsibility on online platforms to protect users and non-compliance can incur penalties including fines and/or imprisonment. Among these responsibilities platforms must take proactive measures to prevent the dissemination of harmful content, this can include indecent images, hate speech and other illegal material (Online Safety Act, 2023; Part 3, Chapter 2). Platforms are also required to implement stringent measures to protect children from online harmful content interactions; this includes the completion of risk and access assessments. Platforms are also required to have mechanisms to swiftly report and address harmful content (Online Safety Act 2023; Part 4, Chapter 2).

The pace at which the Online Safety Act is enacted and enforced will be important in shaping the extent to which, through legal regulation, big tech and online platforms can be held to account for allowing their services to be used by those who offend. The extent to which the law can be applied to those who offend is necessarily limited by the resources of law enforcement. Using the law to regulate those with the power to control online content is the next, and many think overdue, step. While concerns about free speech and the unintended consequences of regulation have understandably acted as checks on intervention, that so much obviously harmful and illegal material litters the mainstream Internet is a tragedy. Social media may be a great enabler of communication, but it is also a largely unregulated paradise for the predator. The Online Safety Bill 2023 has the potential to ease some of the inertia from content providers and platforms to do their part in keeping everyone safe and for the law to hold them to account.

Proportionality and public interest in content between children

The sharing of sexual content, including sexual or nude images of children among themselves, is a complex topic for law enforcement and safeguarding more broadly, especially in education.

The law permits a proportionate response. The fact that a particular act amounts to an offence in law does not necessarily mean that a person should be criminalised. Indeed, sexting between children or sharing of youth produced sexual imagery should not routinely be prosecuted, and most such incidents will be dealt with informally. However, the law is generally equally applicable to children from the age of 10 through to adults, and all of the circumstances will be relevant. For example, where there is coercion, exploitation, grooming or bullying, the position may be different. Factors such as age and age difference, maturity, any response to previous interventions, the extent of any harm caused, mental health and neurodivergence might all be relevant.

This flexibility is necessary given the range of circumstances inevitably arising, but with such flexibility comes uncertainty and the risk of inconsistency. The apparent ubiquity of phones, tablets, social media and online messaging apps among increasingly young people means that online sexualised communication and content among and between children is inevitable. A sensible, proportionate response is available through the discretion of law enforcement, in conjunction with safeguarding leads and guidance from the police, Crown Prosecution Service (CPS) and leading charities, including the National Society for the Prevention of Cruelty to Children (NSPCC) and Barnardo's (see Chapter 8 for information about the Internet Watch Foundation/NSPCC 'Report Remove' tool). However, with this discretion comes a responsibility to act fairly and reasonably in accordance with best practice guidance.

The investigation and prosecution of online child sexual offenders in England and Wales

People who commit online offences come to the attention of the police from a variety of sources including but not limited to:

- A victim of an offence coming forward to report it.
- A complaint resulting from disclosure by or on behalf of a child, such as parents, guardians, social workers or school safeguarding officers.
- Undercover police officers and civilian vigilante groups posing as children online (decoys) and engaging with those who offend on chat sites.
- Established offenders who re-offend on devices monitored by police officers in accordance with a court ordered Sexual Harm Prevention Order (SHPO).
- The National Center for Missing and Exploited Children (NCMEC), an American organisation to which online media companies report instances of child exploitation, including communications, images and abuse.
- Discovery of forensic evidence from others under investigation linking them to the person who has offended.
- Disclosure by wives and family members of evidence discovered on an individual's device.

Many cases of online sexual communication are initiated as a result of child decoys created by law enforcement and civilian vigilante groups, and many investigations relating to indecent images of children result from disclosures by the NCMEC to the National Crime Agency in the UK. A similar scheme is envisaged in the UK with plans for the National Crime Agency, Home Office and Office of Communications (Ofcom) to prepare a similar system (National Crime Agency, 2022).

The volume of unreported online child sexual offences cannot be known. According to the National Police Chief's Council (NPCC), there is significant under-reporting of these crimes. As discussed elsewhere in this book, the use of virtual private networks (VPNs), the dark web, social media and other accounts not linked to email addresses or telephone numbers can impede identifying the person offending. Within the UK alone, the Internet Watch Foundation estimated that during a single month of COVID lockdown in 2020, there were 8.8 million attempts to access child sexual abuse material by internet users (Internet Watch Foundation, 2020). The NPCC (2024) reports on data from 42 UK police forces noting that 107,000 offences of child sexual abuse and exploitation were reported in 2022, nearly quadruple what it was ten years prior.

When an Internet Protocol (IP) address, mobile phone number or email address is linked to online offending, the UK police have an opportunity to identify the perpetrator. Subscriber checks with mobile phone providers and IP address providers are conducted to locate the home or other address of the person who is offending. Preliminary investigations seek to establish how many people live at the address, their gender, whether any of them have criminal records, and if they are subject to the sex offenders register. In cases where it might be difficult to establish who the offender is, the police might apply for a search warrant in court. Where there is reasonable suspicion that a particular individual is responsible, other powers can be relied upon to effect an arrest and/or search.

Arrest and detention

Once an address is identified, a team of police officers, sometimes accompanied by forensic experts or technicians, will attend. Commonly known as "The Knock", such attendances are conducted to secure digital devices that can access the Internet or store images. Where there are sufficient grounds, a person may be arrested and detained at a police station where they will be interviewed. Where grounds are insufficient or due to regional variations in operational procedures, a person will be informed that they are under investigation without being arrested or subject to bail conditions.

Commonly police officers will ask those who are being investigated for the passwords to unlock their devices or passwords or encryption keys to programs and applications. In the event that such a request is refused, officers will consider whether to serve a RIPA notice (s.49 of the Regulation of Investigatory Powers Act 2000). The effect of such a notice will be to compel the disclosure of passwords, etc. Failure to comply with such a notice contrary to s.53 is punishable by up to five years' imprisonment in respect of cases involving national security or child indecency.

In practice, there will be occasions where a person is aware that the police are making an arrest attempt and may panic and delete information or factory reset their devices. Similarly, people might delete the contents of online storage by accessing it from devices not seized by the police. In such cases, there is a risk of being charged with the common law offence of perverting the course of justice. In *R v Sookoo* (2002), the court of appeal cautioned against charging this offence in instances where the behaviour could be treated as an aggravating feature to the main offence. Concealing or destroying evidence is a specific aggravating feature to certain online sexual offences. In instances where a police investigation is wholly thwarted by such destruction, it is likely that serious consideration will be given to charging an offence of perverting the course of justice.

Persons who have been arrested and interviewed are released either on bail or under investigation. Where police officers can impose bail conditions, a person under suspicion might be subject to such restrictions. Practices throughout England and Wales vary, but generally a person under investigation might be prohibited from having unsupervised contact with children, deleting their internet history or possessing devices that can access the Internet unless they notify the police.

Regardless of whether a person under suspicion is released on bail or under investigation, the police investigation will take many months as officers await the results of a forensic analysis of seized devices. A wait of 6–18 months is not uncommon, and periods of 2–3 years (or even more) can occur in cases where there are complications. These might relate to the quantity or nature of devices, a need to identify victims, the interaction of other allegations or particular strains on policing resources locally, especially access to digital forensic resources.

Forensic analysis and reporting

On completion of the forensic analysis, reports are sent to the investigating police officer (see Chapter 4 for a breakdown of the common terms within a forensic report). These reports record the number of image matches to the UK Child Abuse Image Database (CAID), a vital tool that enables forensic software to automatically match images on the suspect's device to known images on the database. Manual investigations may be undertaken to identify newly generated images constantly uploaded to the Internet. Reports also contain keyword results to determine if the suspect has used known search terms, visited certain websites or engaged in conversations with others.

In cases where a person is under suspicion of having sexually communicated with a child and where the child is a decoy created by an undercover officer or civilian vigilante group, the forensic analysis will attempt to retrieve the chat conversations routinely screenshotted by the undercover officer or vigilante group.

The investigation generally culminates when the investigating officer asks or requires the suspect for an interview. If there is no evidence or the evidence does not support a reasonable prospect of conviction, the police or the CPS will take no further action. In some cases where the evidence does not support a criminal conviction but may identify a risk of harm, the police may make an application for a Sexual Risk Order (Sexual Offences Act, 2003 s122). Such orders are prohibitive and are akin to SHPO discussed elsewhere in this chapter.

Where there is a reasonable prospect of conviction, a prosecution will almost always ensue. It is generally in the public interest to prosecute those involved in online child sexual offences. However, in a small number of cases, such as where the person who has offended is a child themselves or is in some way impaired or disordered, or where there is particular mitigation available, an alternative disposal, such as a caution, might be considered.

Prosecution and sentencing

Following positive CPS advice, suspects are charged at the police station if on bail or receive a written requisition to appear at a local Magistrates' Court if under investigation. This hearing generally takes place around one month after receipt of the charges or requisition.

The CPS liaises with the police to ensure they have all of the necessary evidence and material in the case. It will identify the key evidence to be relied upon and manage the other material as necessary. Part of that task is to provide an Initial Details of the Prosecution Case (IDPC) evidential package for the defendant or their legal representatives. The IDPC includes a summary of the offence circumstances, any account given by the defendant in interview, written witness statements and exhibits, and a copy of the defendant's criminal record. In online child sexual offences, the defendant and their solicitors will usually require a copy of the Streamlined Forensic Report (SFR) to assess the strength of the evidence prior to entering a plea (see Chapter 4 for a description of this report and its key contents).

The first hearing at the Magistrates' Court seeks to establish the defendant's plea and the appropriate venue, i.e. whether the case should remain in the Magistrates' Court or be sent to the Crown Court. The Magistrates' powers of sentence are more restricted than those of the Crown Court, leading to most online child sexual offending cases being sent to the Crown Court. The Magistrates also have the discretion to send factually or legally complex cases to the Crown Court. This hearing takes place in public, and the CPS will summarise the case against the defendant in open court.

If a defendant pleads not guilty, their case will be adjourned for a trial, either in the Magistrates Court or in the Crown Court. In Crown Court cases, the trial might occur 9–18 months later, or even longer in some cases. If the defendant pleads guilty (or is later found guilty after a trial), their case will usually be adjourned for about four to eight weeks for a sentencing hearing. This adjournment allows the court time to ensure that all of the necessary information about the defendant is available and to ensure that the right court has enough time to consider the case fully.

Sentencing guidelines

The purpose of sentencing was first enshrined in statutory law in 2003 (Criminal Justice Act, 2003 s142), and it is now incorporated into the Sentencing Act 2020. For those over 18, the court must consider the purposes of sentencing, including the punishment of those who offend, reduction of crime (including by deterrence), reform and rehabilitation, protection of the public and reparation by those who offend to those affected by their offences.

For those under 18, the principal aim of the youth justice system is to prevent offending or re-offending, emphasising reform and rehabilitation while not excluding other measures (Sentencing Act, 2000 s58). When a person is found guilty, they are sentenced by the court – by either a lay bench of Magistrates, a District Judge in the Magistrates' Court, or a Circuit Judge or Recorder in the Crown Court.

Prior to the Criminal Justice Act 2003, a body of case law developed in UK appellate courts established principles of sentencing and guidance on particular cases. This was cumbersome for practitioners who might have to have read a number of judgements in order to determine sentencing ranges. This was compounded by frequent updates and cases being qualified or even overturned by later judgements. This inevitably resulted in inconsistency and unfairness. The Sentencing Council for England and Wales was created to prepare guidelines in order to promote greater consistency in sentencing while maintaining judicial independence. Guidelines are available on the Sentencing Council's website (n.d) which also aims to increase public understanding of sentencing.

Assessing offence seriousness

A sentencing court seeks to establish the seriousness of an offence, determined by the levels of culpability and harm. By way of example, in a case of Sexual Communication with a Child (Sentencing Council, 2022), harm might be higher if sexual images were sent during the communication. Culpability might be higher if the person who offended also made threats or targeted a particularly vulnerable child. Where harm levels might be described numerically and culpability alphabetically, an offence might be categorised as Category 1 harm with Culpability A (Cat 1A), while less serious offences might be Category 1B or Category 2A. The least serious offences might be described as Category 2B. The ranges of harm and culpability vary depending on the offence but seldom go beyond harm categories 1–3 and culpability categories A–C. This type of language has become commonplace in the Criminal Justice System. The clarity for legal professionals might be welcome, but the language can sometimes appear bewildering and characterless.

For example, in a case of causing or inciting a child to engage in sexual activity, Category 1 harm will include cases where there has been penetration, Category 2 where there has been touching or exposure of naked genitalia, and Category 3 will be other sexual activity. Culpability A might include grooming behaviour, abuse of trust or a significant disparity in age. Culpability B relates to factors not included in Culpability A. This categorisation, generally common to all guidelines, permits a sentencing court to establish a starting point and sentencing range, resulting in a level of consistency such that experienced lawyers can accurately estimate likely sentence ranges. Complications arise when people who offend are convicted of multiple offences or offences involving several or more victims. Some practitioners complain of artificiality and the likelihood that strict adherence to the guidelines can result in unfair sentences.

Using the example above, for a Category 1A offence, the starting point is five years' custody, with a range of four to ten years' custody. A Category 3B offence has a starting point of a medium-level community order with a category range of low-level community order to high-level community order. Judges typically stay within the range but may step out of the range based on factors which either aggravate the offence (such as multiple victims or a breach of trust) or might mitigate the offence (such as impairments or disorders linked to the offending). The guidelines give examples of factors which aggravate and mitigate different offences, but there is no closed list.

Aggravating and mitigating factors

Aggravating factors, such as previous relevant convictions, can increase sentences, while mitigating factors, such as remorse or lack of prior convictions, can reduce them. Common statutory aggravating factors might include the commission of offences on bail, racial or religious hostility, etc. Offence-specific aggravating features might include grooming behaviour, the taking or dissemination of photographs of victims, abuse of trust or a significant age disparity between the offender and the victim. A combination of aggravating factors or a particularly serious aggravating fact might result in a significant increase in the starting point for a sentence.

Delays between apprehension and conviction may lead to sentence reductions if not caused by the person who has offended. Those individuals who take steps to address their offending behaviour in the potentially significant wait between apprehension and sentence may benefit from reduced sentences, particularly if they have been abstinent from further offending and have taken demonstrable steps to address their offending behaviour, such as engaging in a therapeutic programme.

Reduction in sentence for guilty plea

Those who plead guilty at the earliest opportunity can expect a one-third reduction in their sentence in most cases. There is a sliding scale, such that delay in entering a guilty plea will result in reduced credit. A guilty plea on the first day of trial will result in a 10% reduction. There will be no reduction where a person is found guilty after trial.

Custody and alternatives

Perhaps one of the more complex matters is determining whether an online sexual offender will go to prison, receive a suspended sentence order or receive a community order. Once again there is a guideline for sentencing judges to consider (Sentencing Council, 2017). There is often a matter of balancing factors that tend towards immediate custody and factors that tend away from it. Those individuals whom the sentencing judge considers a risk of harm or who have previously breached court orders might be more in peril of an immediate custodial sentence. On the other hand, those who can satisfy the sentencing court that there is a reasonable prospect of rehabilitation, or those who have strong personal mitigation or significant caring responsibilities, might be more likely to retain their liberty.

Sometimes the nature of the case might mean that appropriate punishment can only be achieved by immediate custody. Even strongly positive factors indicating an alternative sentence might have little sway. In other cases, even though an offence might easily cross the custody threshold, the just sentence may be a community order.

A suspended sentence order means a person receives a prison sentence but does not go to prison. Instead, they must stay out of further trouble and must usually complete various requirements in the community, such as community service or rehabilitation activities. If the person stays out of trouble and completes their requirements over the period fixed by the court, then they will have completed their sentence. However, if the person commits a further offence or breaches any community requirement, they must serve their prison sentence in custody. The maximum length of sentence that can be suspended is a two-year prison sentence. Therefore, if the court settles on a sentence of more than two years in all the circumstances, the defendant will usually have to go to prison.

However, many of the guidelines with respect to sexual offending make provision for occasions where a sentencing court considers that there is a sufficient prospect of rehabilitation. In such cases, a community order with a sex offender treatment programme can be a proper alternative to a short or moderate-length custodial sentence (Sentencing Act, 2020). Recent jurisprudence from the Court of Appeal suggests that it is open to a sentencing judge to impose a community order where a sentence in excess of two years might otherwise be imposed (R v Liam Driver, 2023). The court observed that the longer the custodial sentence would be – and therefore, the more serious the offence – the stronger the prospect of rehabilitation will need to be in order to justify the imposition of a community order, instead of an immediate custodial sentence.

It is, therefore, perfectly possible in law for a defendant to have committed offences, the behaviour of which is serious enough to warrant a significant prison sentence but for which they receive a sentence which is not immediate imprisonment. It might be that the court concludes that while the sentencing guidelines indicate their behaviour merits a prison term, the just sentence overall, taking into account all of the aggravating and mitigating circumstances, any guilty plea and whether an immediate prison sentence is necessary, is a suspended sentence order or a community order. The court can sometimes give weight to all the aims of sentencing through such orders, with punishment being achieved through unpaid work in the community, electronically monitored tagged curfews and fines. Rehabilitation might be achieved through a sex offender treatment programme being mandated alongside supervision by a probation officer for several years. Prevention of further offending and deterrence might be achieved by leaving a suspended sentence hanging over the defendant, lest they re-offend.

On the other hand, in a different case a court might judge that a defendant's behaviour is so serious that only immediate imprisonment will do. That defendant might have strong mitigation, or the consequences of imprisonment might be severe, but a court must nonetheless send them into prison.

The sentencing guidelines bring consistency and clarity, but a court retains the discretion to impose a sentence that is just.

Notification requirements and sexual harm prevention orders

In addition to determining the substantive sentence, a sentencing court will also have regard to a number of other regimes. As a matter of course, those who commit online child sexual offences will be made subject to the Notification Requirements, otherwise colloquially known as the "Sex Offenders Register". This places restrictions on any person convicted of any offence listed in Schedule 3 of the Sexual Offences Act 2003. There are a small number of exclusions relating to children who offend or those who receive a community order in respect of certain offences. The period someone is made subject to the requirements is set by statute and is determined by the nature and length of sentence. The shortest period for an adult offender is five years. The longest period is for life, with an option to apply for discharge after 15 years (Sexual Offences Act, 2003 s82).

A person subject to the notification requirements must report certain changes in their circumstances to their local police public protection unit (PPU) or its equivalent. Such changes will include changes of name or address, travel abroad and living in a household with a person under the age of 18. The penalty for not reporting such changes can include a prison sentence of up to five years.

A parallel scheme involves the imposition of an SHPO which contains prohibitions on certain behaviours. Such orders are not meant to be punitive and are imposed only in circumstances where the court considers an order is necessary to protect the public from sexual harm (Sentencing Act, 2020 s346). Accordingly, those convicted of sexual communication offences and similar might find themselves subject to a prohibition that they are not permitted unsupervised contact with any person under the age of 18. The order might be limited to restricting online communications to persons under 18 or restrictions according to gender. Those convicted of indecent images offences might be prohibited from using internet-enabled devices unless they notify such use to the police. There may be a provision for the police to install monitoring software, and the individual might be prohibited from deleting internet history. SHPOs may be imposed for a minimum period of five years or any period that the court considers necessary or until further order. The penalty for breaching an SHPO is a maximum term of imprisonment of five years (Sentencing Act, 2000, s354).

Online child sexual offences where there is no identifiable victim

The sentencing of offences where it is not known whether a real child was involved or where it is known that a police or civilian decoy was used has caused a challenge to the criminal justice system over a number of years. Many considered that such cases resulted in the imposition of lenient sentences in the English and Welsh courts. When evaluating harm and culpability, complications arose when an individual communicated sexually with an adult posing as a child. The real harm caused in such cases is arguably minimal or non-existent, even though the culpability or blameworthiness is the same. Nonetheless, while encouraging a fictional child to engage in sexual activity is less harmful than inciting a real child, many believe the punishment should be the same or similar on the basis that the intention was the same.

Consider a case where an adult male contacts an undercover police officer who is posing as a 12-year-old female. Unaware he is speaking to an officer, the offender arranges to meet and engage in sexual intercourse. According to the Attorney General's Reference (Baker, 2014), the appropriate charge would be under section 10 of the Sexual Offences Act 2003 for causing or inciting a child to engage in sexual activity. The sentencing court must assess harm and culpability, but because the offence did not go beyond incitement and there was no sexual intercourse with the child (there never could have been), it was classified as "other sexual activity" within Category 3.

These cases involving decoy profiles were often deemed low harm but high culpability, i.e. Cat3A offences. Sentences typically started at six months' imprisonment and ranged from high-level community orders to three years' imprisonment. Offenders entering an early guilty plea might receive a suspended sentence or community order.

However, a significant change occurred with the case of *R v Privett* (2020). The court ruled that judges should identify harm based on the intended sexual activity, then adjust the sentence to be proportionate if no actual activity occurred. This led to categorising such cases as Category 1 harm (intended penetration) and Cat A culpability, significantly increasing the starting point to five years' imprisonment, with a range of four to ten years. A minor reduction could be applied if there was no real victim, but offenders faced around three to four years' imprisonment with an early guilty plea.

Further changes came in 2022 (Police Crime Sentencing and Courts Act, 2022 s46), which allowed arranging or facilitating a child sexual offence under section 14 of the Sexual Offences Act 2003 to include more serious crimes. Consequently, a person who has arranged or facilitated a penetrative child sexual offence with a decoy posing as a child under 13 might have received a suspended sentence or even a community order in 2018. However, that same person would now face a starting point of 16 years' imprisonment, with a range of 13–19 years. Additionally, the same act requires offenders sentenced after June 2022 to serve two-thirds of their sentence before release, rather than half (Police, Crime, Sentencing and Courts Act, 2022, s130).

This updated approach to dealing with cases involving decoys or where there is no real child is now fully reflected in the current sentencing guidelines and reflects what is said to be Parliament's intention in defining 'harm' as including harm caused or intended. Put otherwise, a person offending in this way does not get away lightly because, unbeknownst to them, the person on the other end of the messaging is not who they seem.

Conclusions

The law presents a plethora of available offences to cover online sexual offending. In spite of the challenges presented by developing technology and ever more sophisticated offenders, the legal framework offers a comprehensive range of tools to law enforcement and prosecutors. The Online Safety Act 2023 has meaningfully added to that toolkit, not only with some additional offences but also with a fresh emphasis on the responsibility of content and platform providers. While the criminal justice system for dealing with these offences creaks under the weight of caseload and ever more strained resources, the depth and thoroughness of investigations has led to record numbers of prosecutions and convictions, which are met with ever tougher sentences.

Overall, both the legal framework and the legal system in practice have enough scope and flexibility to meet most of the demands of the present day. The length of time investigations take to be resolved is a scandal for all concerned, especially when a trial or contested issues arise. A level of justice can be expected, but only after a considerable wait at best.

As we go forward, it might be thought that the relevance of the distinction between online offending or otherwise is fading in legal significance. The blurring of the lines between the real world and the online world, if they have ever really existed, is being increasingly reflected in the approach of the legal framework. Those who offend behind the keyboard or keypad, scrolling, sharing and clicking leave real victims in the real world.

References

Children Act 1989, s.105. https://www.legislation.gov.uk/ukpga/1989/41/section/105

Coroners and Justice Act 2009, s.62. https://www.legislation.gov.uk/ukpga/2009/25/section/62

Criminal Justice Act 1988, s.160. https://www.legislation.gov.uk/ukpga/1988/33/section/160#:~:text=160%20%5BF1Possession%20of%20indecent,.%20.%20.%20in%20his%20possession.

Criminal Justice Act 2003, s142. https://www.legislation.gov.uk/ukpga/2003/44/section/142/enacted

Criminal Justice and Immigration Act 2008, p. 5. https://www.legislation.gov.uk/ukpga/2008/4/part/5#:~:text=63Possession%20of%20extreme%20pornographic,of%20an%20extreme%20pornographic%20image.&text=(b)an%20extreme%20image

Internet Watch Foundation. (May 2020). *Millions of attempts to access child sexual abuse online during lockdown.* Retrieved 6 July 2024 from https://webarchive.nationalarchives.gov.uk/ukgwa/20221215020934/https://www.iicsa.org.uk/key-documents/28700/view/INQ006766.pdf

Internet Watch Foundation. (October 2023). *How AI is being abused to create child sexual abuse imagery.* Retrieved 6 June 2024 from https://www.iwf.org.uk/about-us/why-we-exist/our-research/how-ai-is-being-abused-to-create-child-sexual-abuse-imagery/#:~:text=Report%20summary&text=The%20key%20findings%20of%20this,most%20likely%20to%20be%20criminal

National Crime Agency. (March 2022). *New reporting regime for online child sexual abuse content announced.* Retrieved 6 July 2024 from https://www.nationalcrimeagency.gov.uk/news/new-reporting-regime-for-online-child-sexual-abuse-content-announced

National Police Chief's Council. (January 2024). *Child sexual abuse and exploitation analysis launched.* Retrieved 6 July 2024 from https://news.npcc.police.uk/releases/vkpp-launch-national-analysis-of-police-recorded-child-sexual-abuse-and-exploitation-csae-crimes-report-2022

Online Safety Act 2023, part 3, chapter 2. https://www.legislation.gov.uk/ukpga/2023/50/part/3/chapter/2

Online Safety Act 2023, part 4, chapter 2. https://www.legislation.gov.uk/ukpga/2023/50/part/4/chapter/2

Police Crime Sentencing and Courts Act 2022, s46. https://www.legislation.gov.uk/ukpga/2022/32/section/46/enacted

Police Crime Sentencing and Courts Act 2022, s130. https://www.legislation.gov.uk/ukpga/2022/32/section/130

Protection of Children Act 1978, https://www.legislation.gov.uk/ukpga/1978/37

Protection of Children Act 1978, s1. https://www.legislation.gov.uk/ukpga/1989/41/section/1

Protection of Children Act 1978, s.7. https://www.legislation.gov.uk/ukpga/1978/37/section/7#:~:text=7%20Interpretation.&text=(3)Photographs%20(including%20those,as%20respects%20pseudo%2Dphotographs%5D.

Regina v Baker. (2014). EWCA Crim 2752. https://www.5pumpcourt.com/media/fhjfroen/attorney-general-s-reference-no-94-of-2014.pdf

Regina v DM. (2011). EWCA Crim 2752. https://www.bailii.org/ew/cases/EWCA/Crim/2011/2752.html

Regina v. Graham-Kerr. (1989). 88 Cr App R 302. https://vlex.co.uk/vid/r-v-graham-kerr-793639121

Regina v Jayson. (2003). Cr App R 13. https://vlex.co.uk/vid/r-v-smith-graham-793762225

Regina v Land. (1998). 1 Cr App R 301. https://vlex.co.uk/vid/r-v-land-michael-793737809

Regina v Liam Driver. (2023). EWCA Crim 434.

Regina v. Neal. (2011). EWCA Crim 461. https://www.bailii.org/ew/cases/EWCA/Crim/2011/461.html

Regina v Okoro. (2018). EWCA Crim 1929. https://vlex.co.uk/vid/possession-in-the-digital-874307522

Regina v Privett and others. (2020). EWCA Crim 557. https://www.bailii.org/ew/cases/EWCA/Crim/2020/557.html

Regina v Sookoo. (2002). EWCA Crim 800. https://vlex.co.uk/vid/r-v-sookoo-792829829

Sentencing Act 2020, part 3. https://www.legislation.gov.uk/ukpga/2020/17/schedule/16/part/3

Sentencing Act 2020, section 58. https://www.legislation.gov.uk/ukpga/2020/17/section/58#:~:text=58Offenders%20aged%20under%2018%3A%20considerations%20of%20court%20not%20affected%20by%20Code&text=(a)to%20have%20regard%20to,and%20Disorder%20Act%201998)%3B

Sentencing Act 2020, section 346. https://www.legislation.gov.uk/ukpga/2020/17/section/346/2022-04-28

Sentencing Act 2020, section 354. https://www.legislation.gov.uk/ukpga/2020/17/section/354

Sentencing Council. (n.d). https://www.sentencingcouncil.org.uk/

Sentencing Council. (2014). *Possession of indecent photograph of child/indecent photographs of Children*. Retrieved on 6 June from https://www.sentencingcouncil.org.uk/offences/magistrates-court/item/possession-of-indecent-photograph-of-child/

Sentencing Council. (February 2017). *Imposition of community and custodial sentences*. Retrieved 6 July 2024 from https://www.sentencingcouncil.org.uk/overarching-guides/crown-court/item/imposition-of-community-and-custodial-sentences/

Sentencing Council. (July 2022). *Sexual communication with a child*. Retrieved 6 July 2024 from https://www.sentencingcouncil.org.uk/offences/crown-court/item/sexual-communication-with-a-child/

Sexual Offences Act 2003, https://www.legislation.gov.uk/ukpga/2003/42/contents

Sexual Offences Act 2003, s8. https://www.legislation.gov.uk/ukpga/2003/42/section/8

Sexual Offences Act 2003, s10. https://www.legislation.gov.uk/ukpga/2003/42/section/10

Sexual Offences Act 2003, s12. https://www.legislation.gov.uk/ukpga/2003/42/section/12
Sexual Offences Act 2003, s14. https://www.legislation.gov.uk/ukpga/2003/42/section/14
Sexual Offences Act 2003, s15. https://www.legislation.gov.uk/ukpga/2003/42/section/15
Sexual Offences Act 2003, s66. https://www.legislation.gov.uk/ukpga/2003/42/section/66
Sexual Offences Act 2003, s82. https://www.legislation.gov.uk/ukpga/2003/42/section/82
Sexual Offences Act 2003, s122. https://www.legislation.gov.uk/ukpga/2003/42/section/122

7 Forensic risk assessment of online offending

Ruth J Tully

Introduction

This chapter discusses some of the commonly used risk tools used by psychologists that relate to sexual, stalking and extremism-based offending and if or how these take into account online methods of offending.

Sexual offending risk assessment

As the reader will be well aware, sexual offending is a massive problem in society. Over recent years, the empirical literature in this field has focused on effective risk assessment of individuals. Over time, various tools have been developed to aid clinicians in their assessments, which can broadly be separated into two categories: static/actuarial tools and dynamic risk tools.

Static risk assessment

Static or actuarial methods use algorithms and give probabilistic estimates of risk. There are few tools designed to specifically assess risk for those with indecent image offences. The Child Pornography Offender Risk Tool (CPORT; Seto & Eke, 2015) is an actuarial tool developed for use with this population, and it considers the following:

- The age of the offender
- Prior criminal history
- Failure on conditional release
- Contact sexual offending
- Evidence of paedophilia (including consideration of the Correlates of Admitted Sexual Interest in Children (CASIC) tool, described below)
- Preference for male victims

The CASIC scale requires an assessor to determine:

- Whether an online sexual offender has ever been married
- Whether they had videos of child abuse in their possession

DOI: 10.4324/9781003543794-7

- Whether they had text stories of child abuse in their possession
- Whether their online offending lasted two or more years
- Whether they have volunteered in a role with high access to children
- Whether they engaged in online communication with a minor or decoy

Whilst the CASIC is not recommended as a stand-alone measure of sexual interest in children, the above risk markers can assist in exploring the breadth of an individual's online behaviour. Although the CPORT was not found to predict re-offending for men with indecent image offences only (Seto & Eke, 2015), validation studies with Canadian samples found that it predicted the sexual re-offending of indecent image offenders for contact and non-contact offences (Eke et al., 2018). Another actuarial tool, the Risk Matrix 2000 (Thornton et al., 2003), was developed initially for offline offending. It is generally well validated (e.g. Helmus et al., 2013), but this tool has been found to overestimate risk for online sexual offenders. An adapted version of this tool with some items removed was more promising (Osborn et al., 2010).

Not necessarily applied by psychologists but relevant to discuss due to its wide-scale use within prison and probation services in England and Wales, is the OASys OSP/I (Offender Assessment System, OASys Sexual Predictor/I), which is designed to assess the likelihood of re-offending for those convicted of indecent images of children offences (but not 'extreme pornography' or other non-contact offending). There is also an OASys Sexual Predictor/C (OSP/C) designed to assess the risk of future contact sexual offences. The OSP/C was found to be slightly more predictive (of proven contact sexual offending) than the Risk Matrix 2000 in one study (Howard & Wakeling, 2021). As a result of this and the simplicity of the OSP, the routine application of Risk Matrix 2000 in prison and probation services in England and Wales was dropped in favour of the use of OSP. The OSP/I is calculated automatically within OASys based on very basic information: 'low' risk = no sanctions for indecent images of children offences, 'medium' = one sanction for indecent images of children offences, and 'high' = more than one sanction for indecent images of children offences. The OSP/I provides practitioners with the rates of proven indecent images of children offences within the validation sample (low = 0.3%, medium = 2.8% and high = 5.8%) to assist them in their risk analysis of an individual. More recently, OSP/C was found to underpredict contact sexual reoffending (Craik et al., 2024) and as a result OSP/C and OSP/I were further examined by Emeagi et al. (2024). They found that model performance varied based on the type of sexual reoffending, particularly those involving online contact been the offender and a victim ('indirect contact child offences'). Several changes to both OSP/C and OSP/I were proposed resulting on two suggested modified predictors; OSP Direct Contact (OSP/DC; designed as it sounds to predict direct sexual contact offences) and OSP Indecent images and Indirect Contact (OSP/IIC; designed to predict indecent images of children and/or indirect contact child offences). The OSP/IIC remains a simple algorithm that only considers past history of sexual offending, but this now includes indirect contact child offences as well as indecent images offences (Emeagi et al., 2024) and was planned to be implemented within prison and probation services following Emeagi and colleagues' publication of results (MoJ, 2024).

As mentioned, the CPORT, Risk Matrix 2000 and OSP/I or OSP/IIC are actuarial tools which, by their nature, do not tell us about the psychological, dynamic risk factors associated with sexual risk. It is generally accepted in the field of forensic risk assessment that a comprehensive assessment will also consider a range of dynamic, changeable factors. These dynamic factors contribute to an overall view of the risk of sexual offending, and assessing the risk of online sexual offending is no exception.

Dynamic risk assessment

Structured professional judgement-based methods involve the assessor considering the presence and relevance of identified risk factors. These risk factors are then considered within an individually tailored psychological formulation. The purpose of the clinical case formulation is to consider issues such as the predisposing, precipitating, perpetuating, and protective factors associated with the behaviour of concern. The dynamic risk assessment process leads to the development of possible future risk scenarios (i.e. if re-offending occurred, what this might look like), an overall risk judgement (e.g. low, moderate, high) with consideration of important features such as imminence of risk and warning signs, and accompanying risk management plans for the offender, and any victim-specific risk management strategies (see Webster et al., 2013, for an overview of this process).

There is no structured professional judgement-based sexual risk tool specifically designed for online sexual offenders. Additionally, we know that indecent images offences are just one form of online sexual offending, which can include grooming or psychological coercion of victims with the aim of committing contact offences and other forms of offending, such as the sharing of private images without consent. Sexual offenders are a heterogeneous group, as are victims who could have any relationship to the perpetrator, e.g. stranger, intimate partner, child, adult or acquaintance. Widely used structured professional judgement tools such as RSVPv2 (Hart et al., 2022) and SVR-20v2 (Boer et al., 2018) are designed with the flexibility to consider offending that is entirely or partially committed online. The definitions of sexual offending contained within these tools include online sexual offending, not limited to indecent images, and the tools' manuals contain guidance on how to consider these behaviours and implications for risk. This allows for scenario generation and risk management planning to occur for possible future risk situations, which can include online sexual offending risk consideration.

Often, services are interested in the risk of 'crossover' offending; this term refers to the risk of someone who has committed online sexual offending crossing over to contact sexual offending. There is no reliable way of assessing the risk of crossover, and no risk tool claims to be able to 'predict' this. Some literature suggests key differences between those who offend online only and those with contact/ mixed offences. However, there remains no reliable way to tell if the person you assess will cross over. The literature does not support the idea that all those with online sexual offences will cross over. However, the reality is that some people do, which poses a problem for risk assessment, especially in light of the suggestion that those who do crossover are a particularly high-risk group (Babchishin et al., 2015).

Furthermore, consideration needs to be given by assessors to potential 'crossover' or diversification from contact sexual offending to online sexual offending; in some cases, those with strict reporting and community conditions around access to children may be motivated to sexually offend online as it can seem easier to satisfy a sexual interest in children with what they may consider a lower likelihood of detection this way for them. This has occurred in several cases in which I have been involved. Therefore, risk assessors need to give careful consideration to both online and offline sexual offending as part of a robust risk assessment.

Stalking risk assessment

Stalking can (and commonly does) occur in both the offline and online worlds. The Internet gives the person engaged in a stalking episode a vast resource through which they can research, communicate with, and communicate about a person. Harassment and stalking can be done online with less physical effort, and the Internet can afford the perpetrator some perceived, and possibly actual, anonymity in their stalking behaviours (see Chapter 2 for more information).

Two common risk assessment tools used for stalking risk are the Stalking Risk Profile (SRP; MacKenzie et al., 2009) and Stalking Assessment and Management version 2 (SAMv2; Kropp et al., 2023). Both tools operate from the perspective that in order to understand a case, the assessor must understand stalking motivation. Both tools employ a structured professional judgement approach, as described above. However, these tools have some procedural differences; one being at what point within the assessment motivation for stalking should be determined. In the SAMv2, the motivation is drawn from assessment of the presence and relevance of risk factors and an individual clinical case formulation. In the SRP, the motivation for stalking is determined from the start of the assessment, and the assessor is guided by the tool's instructions to classify the 'type' of stalker being assessed (rejected, resentful, intimacy-seeking, incompetent and predatory), based on their primary motivation and the literature on the typology of stalking (Mullen et al., 1999). The identified 'type' then affects the set of risk actors that should be considered in the specific case.

Another difference between these tools relates to the structure of the risk judgement. Other notable differences are that the SAMv2 contains a domain that specifically considers victim vulnerabilities that might place a person at increased risk of stalking victimisation, and the SRP does not. Additionally, the SRP contains a section on risk assessment for the stalking of public figures/celebrities, whereas the SAMv2 does not. In practice, both tools can provide a comprehensive assessment of stalking risk, but it should be acknowledged that neither was specifically designed for online stalking and harassment. With that said, both tools allow flexible consideration of all stalking behaviours, including online and offline behaviours, to inform the risk assessment and management considerations. It is down to assessors to be alert to potential methods of stalking behaviour and to plan for future scenarios that may include online facilitated stalking, whether or not the person has engaged in this form of stalking before.

A further consideration with online stalking, which, although is present with offline stalking, may not be present to the same degree, is that victims and criminal justice services may be completely unaware of the extent of the online stalking behaviour if this is well hidden by the perpetrator. Behaviour could, for example, involve repetitive and obsessional viewing of someone's photographs on social media, which could escalate to unwanted messages and contact. The messages and contact may be fairly easily evidenced. However, if the perpetrator success-fully conceals their history of internet use, the obsessional research and looking at images of the person online may go unnoticed. There can also be difficulties in detecting stalking re-offending if perpetrated by the individual entirely online unless there is a robust risk management plan in place that monitors online behav-iour effectively. It may, therefore, in some cases be relevant and proportionate that the offenders' licence conditions (if subject to a licence) include conditions around the monitoring of devices and internet use, even if their stalking behaviours have previously been entirely offline in the past. Otherwise, critical analysis and moni-toring of avenues of risk escalation and offending can be missed.

Extremism/terrorism offending risk assessment

There are various aspects of online and offline activity to consider within the field of risk assessment for terrorism-related offending. For instance, it is important to attempt to discriminate between those who are the target of others attempting to radicalise or recruit them and those who are disseminating terrorism-related mate-rials or inciting violent extremism. It is also important to consider who may be likely to cross over from online incitement to actually planning or carrying out violent extremist acts. Indeed, there will also be people who do not engage in online incitement who engage in violent action. However, none of this discrimi-nation between types of extremist risk can be done with certainty. As with other types of risk (e.g. sexual), risk assessment of violent extremism can be informed by information obtained from internet content alongside other observed behaviour and collateral information. In fact, online evidence, whether from social media or messages between people/groups, often provides valuable evidence for both pros-ecution and risk assessment.

The reach of the Internet has influenced the adoption of extremist ideology world-wide, and it is also the case that some groups specifically and deliberately use online communication and propaganda to radicalise people and recruit them to their 'cause'. Unfortunately, this has also resulted in vulnerable young people and adults being tar-geted online and subsequently used by groups for extremist offending. It is also the case that those who may not be particularly vulnerable can still become influenced and more extreme in their beliefs by being flooded with online information that may be inaccurate or incomplete. Terrorist groups have, over time, become more adept and creative with their methods of recruitment and indoctrination.

Several risk tools are available to aid practitioners in assessing individuals with possible violent extremism risk. These specialist tools typically and appropriately require assessors to receive specialist training. These include ERG22+ (see Lloyd & Dean, 2015; commonly used within prison and probation services in England and Wales), VERA-2R (Pressman et al., 2018; in use in Europe and around the world), MLGv2 (Cook et al., 2015; considers group-based violence including but not limited to terrorism) and TRAP-18 (see Meloy, 2018; considers lone-actor terrorism). Most such tools adopt a structured professional judgement approach to risk assessment, and the evidence used to apply these instruments includes (and indeed benefits from) data regarding the individual's online activity, which will assist in rating the items. For example, I have been involved in cases where online chat content and searches provided valuable evidence of the extent of planning and targets of a violent attack, the roles that each person undertook in planning, the roles they intended to undertake in the attack, and also the language and content of chat provided valuable evidence about their offence-related attitudes. Given that, in this case, the perpetrators later denied the intent and extremist ideology, this online data provided invaluable information about attitudes, psychological treatment needs, and, therefore, also about risk.

Although all digital evidence obtained can be used to inform the rating of items within risk assessment, it is pertinent to highlight that a dedicated cyber risk tool for violent extremism would likely provide enhanced analysis and understanding of the nuances of an individual's risk. However, research in this area is lacking. A relatively recent development is a cyber-specific tool called CYBERA (Pressman & Ivan, 2019) which provides a method of delineating internet activity and a structure for analysis of linguistic and imagery elements. The primary author of the VERA-2R developed the CYBERA, which can be structured into the VERA-2R risk indicators. Systematic and structured consideration of relevant cyber indicators seems likely to enhance risk assessment practice in this area and is an ongoing area of research.

As mentioned, structured professional judgement approaches advocate for scenario planning, where consideration is given to what future offending would look like if it were to reoccur. Therefore, assessors can consider scenarios relevant to the case, which might include online scenarios involving inciting violence or scenarios that may involve actual physical violence perpetration, which are planned for via online means. Enhanced consideration of online data/evidence will assist assessors in generating the most plausible repeat, escalation and twist (which is where something about the offending changes) scenarios so that the most effective and appropriate risk management strategies can be implemented.

Conclusions

The online world provides ever-changing ways of facilitating and committing crime. Risk assessment tools used by psychologists, such as those described in this chapter, consider evidence of online activity alongside other evidence; online evidence can be of central importance to understanding and assessing risk. Although limited tools are designed specifically to assess the risk of offending via online means, most tools, specifically those that take a structured professional judgement approach, allow assessors the flexibility to consider a range of potential future risk scenarios, including online offending. Risk assessors need to be aware of the ever-changing methods of online offending and ways people avoid detection to ensure that risk assessment is comprehensive and that risk management plans are as robust as possible. The limitations of the available tools, mainly around most tools not being explicitly designed for online offending and relevant literature related to online methods of offending, should be kept in mind by assessors.

References

Babchishin, K. M., Hanson, R. K., & VanZuylen, H. (2015). Online child pornography offenders are different: A meta-analysis of the characteristics of online and offline sex offenders against children. *Archives of Sexual Behavior, 44*(1), 45–66.

Boer, D. P., Hart, S. D., Kropp, P. R., & Webster, C. D. (2018). *Manual for Version 2 of the Sexual Violence Risk-20: Structured professional guidelines for assessing and managing risk of sexual violence.* Vancouver: Protect International.

Cook, A. N., Hart, S. D., & Kropp, R. (2015). *Multi-Level Guidelines version 2.* Burnaby: Mental Health, Law, and Policy Institute, Simon Fraser University.

Craik, A., Han, L., Sullivan, L., Landsiedel, J., Travers, T., Spaull, C., & Howard, P. (2024). *Revalidation: Risk of recidivism tools. An evaluation of the actuarial instruments developed to assess recidivism risk in England and Wales.* (Ministry of Justice Analytical Series, unnumbered). London: Ministry of Justice.

Eke, A. W., Helmus, L. M., & Seto, M. C. (2018). A validation study of the Child Pornography Offender Risk Tool (CPORT). *Sexual Abuse, 31*(4), 456–476.

Emeagi, C., Sullivan, L., Landsiedel, J., Craik, A. & Howard, P. (2024). *The actuarial prediction of sexual reoffending: Responding to changing offending patterns. Ministry of Justice Analytical Series.* London: Ministry of Justice.

Hart, S. D., Kropp, P. R., Watt, K. A., Darjee, R., Davis, M. R., Klaver, J., Laws, D. R., & Logan, C. (2022). *RSVP-V2: Version 2 of the Risk for Sexual Violence Protocol.* Vancouver: Protect International.

Helmus, L., Babchishin, K. M. & Hanson, K. R. (2013). The predictive accuracy of the Risk Matrix 2000: A meta-analysis. *Sexual Offender Treatment, 8*(2), 1–20.

Howard, P., & Wakeling, H. (2021). *Comparing two predictors of sexual recidivism; the Risk Matrix 2000 and the OASys Sexual Reoffending Predictor.* London: Ministry of Justice Analytical Series.

Kropp, R., Hart, S. D., & Lyon, D. R. (2023). *Guidelines for stalking assessment and management version 2.* Vancouver: Protect International.

Lloyd, M., & Dean, C. (2015). The development of structured guidelines for assessing risk in extremist offenders. *Journal of Threat Assessment and Management, 2*(1), 40–52.

MacKenzie, R., McEwan, T. E., Pathe, M., James, D. V., Ogloff, J. R., & Mullen, P. E. (2009). *Stalking risk profile: Guidelines for the assessment and management of stalkers.* (1st ed.) Victoria: Monash University.

Meloy, J. R. (2018). The operational development and empirical testing of the Terrorist Radicalization Assessment protocol (TRAP-18). *Journal of Personality Assessment, 100*(5), 483–492.

Ministry of Justice. (2024). *The actuarial prediction of sexual reoffending – Policy addendum.* London: Author.

Mullen, P. E., Pathé, M., Purcell, R., & Stuart, G. W. (1999). Study of stalkers. *The American Journal of Psychiatry, 156,* 1244–1249.

Osborn, J., Elliott, I. A., Middleton, D., & Beech, A. R. (2010). The use of actuarial risk assessment measures with UK internet child pornography offenders. *Journal of Aggression, Conflict, and Peace Research, 2,* 16–24. https://doi.org/10.5042/jacpr.2010.0333

Pressman, D. E., & Ivan, C. (2019). Internet use and violent extremism: A cyber-VERA risk assessment protocol. In M. Khosrow-Pour (Ed.), *Multigenerational online behavior and media use: Concepts, methodologies, tools, and applications* (pp. 266–284). Hershey, PA: Information Science Reference/IGI Global.

Pressman, E., Duits, N., Rinne, T., & Flockton, J. S. (2018). *VERA-2R: Violent extremism risk assessment – Version 2 Revised: A structured professional judgement approach.* Netherlands: Netherlands Institute of Forensic Psychiatry and Psychology (NIFP).

Seto, M. C. & Eke, A. W. (2015). Predicting recidivism among adult male child pornography offenders: Development of the Child Pornography Offender Risk Tool (CPORT). *Law and Human Behavior, 39,* 416–429.

Thornton, D., Mann, R., Webster, S., Blud, L., Travers, R., Friendship, C., & Erikson, M. (2003). Distinguishing and combining risks for sexual and violent recidivism. *Annals of the New York Academy of Sciences, 989,* 225–235.

Webster, C. D., Douglas, K. S., Eaves, D., & Hart, S. D. (2013). *HCR-20 assessing risk for violence version 3.* British Columbia: Mental Health, Law and Policy Institute Simon Fraser University.

8 Emerging approaches to online crime prevention

Christopher Wise and Jennifer Bamford

Introduction

The Internet is a haven for criminals, but it's also a powerful tool for prevention against risky online behaviour. This chapter explores some of the organisations and their strategies to tackle the rise of online offending. It also explores the technological and educational techniques used by world leaders to prevent online offences.

Artificial intelligence and machine learning

As the complexity of online offences increases, the tools and technology used by those protecting the public, particularly children, must also progress. The Internet Watch Foundation (IWF), a highly regarded and influential organisation, is at the forefront of this battle. Established in 1996, this UK charity has grown into a global leader in the reporting, identification and removal of child sexual abuse material (CSAM) from the Internet. Their blending of technology and human expertise ensures that harmful content is swiftly eradicated and reported to law enforcement.

Digital fingerprints

One of the critical requirements for identifying and removing CSAM material at the speed and scale necessary when dealing with something as vast and fast-moving as the Internet is the ability to do it automatically without humans manually intervening and verifying it. So, how do we teach a machine to recognise an image? The answer is through digital fingerprinting; we've discussed file "hashes", the process of using mathematical algorithms to create a unique signature for a file in previous chapters. The IWF maintain and share a database of these digital fingerprints with its members. These members include social media platforms, search engines, Internet service providers and telecom providers. For IWF members using this hash list, it is possible not only to identify CSAM material on their platforms and services but also to block it, further preventing the spread of these images and the harm they cause.

The IWF is not the only organisation working to stop the spread of CSAM material by identifying and hashing these harmful images. The collaboration between

DOI: 10.4324/9781003543794-8

these organisations is crucial in helping unify their efforts; the U.S.-based National Center for Missing and Exploited Children (NCMEC) has created centralised hash-sharing platforms for NGOs and the tech industry. This database is described as being the world's largest quality-assured database of CSAM in the world, consisting of over five million hashes of known images.

One of the challenges of traditional file hashing techniques is that even a slight change to an image will cause the hash to be different. As a result, a CSAM image that has been cropped or altered in even the most minuscule of ways would need to be reported and hashed again. However, technology companies have yet to stop at this hurdle. They have developed new techniques of hashing, known as 'fuzzy' or 'perceptual matching', to identify images consistently regardless of any changes. The most notable is PhotoDNA, developed by Microsoft in partnership with Dartmouth College in 2009 for their search engine Bing (Microsoft, n.d.). Microsoft donated this technology to the National Center for Missing and Exploited Children. In 2015, they also made it available to select customers for free on their cloud platform, Azure. Other similar technologies have been released for free by Google, Meta and, recently, Cloudflare. These technological advancements inspire hope and progress, showing that we are constantly evolving and improving in our fight against online offences and that the efforts are becoming increasingly collaborative.

In 2018, Microsoft made another technological leap forward in identifying CSAM. Previously, for video-based content, analysts needed to watch every video to manually identify CSAM material, regardless of whether it was already known or the first time it had been seen. This analysis would be both time-consuming and challenging. That was until Microsoft released PhotoDNA for video; this new technology, built upon PhotoDNA, can analyse any video, frame by frame, to identify known CSAM. Like its original service, Microsoft offers this service to organisations for free.

Artificial intelligence

The digital fingerprinting approach discussed works only for already identified images and relies on analysts' hard work and efforts to view and validate CSAM; this is a massive and daunting task. One of the recent advancements in the fight against CSAM is the use of artificial intelligence (AI). Given the sheer volume of data to analyse, organisations have developed AI tools that can analyse images at an unprecedented rate, far faster than even a team of humans could do. However, using these tools doesn't remove the human element altogether. No AI is 100% accurate; therefore, a human eye is required to verify the AI findings. However, this reduces the need for a person to sit reviewing potentially thousands of images or hours of video footage, vastly increasing the volume of potential material that one person can review.

In addition to being a helpful tool for identifying and classifying reported CSAM, social media and similar tech platforms that hold or process images can use AI to block potential CSAM proactively. One such AI tool, "Safer" has been created by the not-for-profit organisation Thorn. This tool combines the traditional method of hash matching CSAM to their database of known images and uses state-of-the-art AI to identify new, previously unseen CSAM. In addition to identifying photos, one of the other AI-driven features of the Safer platform is the ability to analyse conversations and identify potential child exploitation.

Another innovative use of AI is a joint campaign between the IWF and the Lucy Faithfull Foundation. The Lucy Faithfull Foundation is a UK child protection charity that works to prevent child sexual abuse. Its approach is to work with people who pose a risk to children by diverting them from causing harm. One of the strategies used by the Lucy Faithfull Foundation involves directing people who offend against children to seek help through targeted advertisements; these ads appear when someone searches for keywords associated with CSAM. The Lucy Faithfull Foundation has been using this approach to divert people who offend online across the clear and dark web. Following the IWF being granted funding by the End Violence Fund to develop a tool to prevent children from becoming victims of sexual abuse, they partnered with the Lucy Faithfull Foundation in the creation of an AI chatbot, reThink, that can be targeted at internet users who are showing signs that they may be looking for CSAM. The reThink chatbot engages them in a "friendly and supportive" conversation to make them realise that their behaviour is damaging to children, directing them to services that can help them change their unhealthy behaviours before they act upon them.

The reThink chatbot was deployed by MindGeek (now Aylo) to their PornHub platform in 2022. It would appear on-screen alongside a warning to all UK users of PornHub that searched for a CSAM-related term. The University of Tasmania (UT) evaluated the chatbot's efficacy and released its findings in February 2024. The evaluation results were positive and demonstrated that when compared to displaying just a warning, there was a statistically significant reduction in continued searches using CSAM keywords (Scanlan et al., 2024).

A deep dive into the UT study results

The study by UT revealed some interesting statistics about the efficacy of the chatbot in connecting users to specialist support; between March 2022 and August 2023, the chatbot was displayed 2.8 million times. Of those, there were 1,656 requests for further information about Stop It Now! by the user and 490 click-throughs to the Stop It Now! website. These click-throughs resulted in 69 calls and chats to the Stop It Now! anonymous counselling service. Of this relatively small group of users who sought support from Stop It Now!, Joel Scanlan and colleagues found five distinct categories:

- *Panic and distress:* Users who were panicked by the warning message, believing they may have been referred to the police or go to prison, and who indicated that they would not interact with pornography again.
- *Tech support:* Users who wanted to get rid of the warning with common emotions of anger and frustration being expressed.

- *Help seekers:* Users who were asking for help to change their behaviour.
- *Information seekers:* Users who wanted more information, expressing disgust at having searched for CSAM and wanting advice on staying safe online.
- *Time wasters:* Users who contacted Lucy Faithfull Foundation to waste time or cause discomfort to Lucy Faithfull staff without interest in support or help.

The sample size of this study was clearly small and had various limitations, including the lack of reliability about whether the data is from different users or the same user across different time periods or from different devices. Additionally, whilst some desistance is reported, it is possible that those who 'desisted' from further CSAM searches were, in fact, desisted from using PornHub as a platform, not desisting from the behaviour itself. It is possible that after receiving the warning, they may then have proceeded to another website to seek out CSAM. Despite these limitations, the authors identify various future developments for the chatbot, including linking the user to other related services, such as The Samaritans, and enabling the chatbot to connect the user directly to a real person from Stop It Now!

Helplines

Stop It Now!, founded in 1992 by child sexual abuse survivor Fran Henry, is an American charity created to have "the sexual abuse of children recognized as a preventable public health problem". In 1995, Stop It Now! launched an anonymous helpline for people at risk of committing child sexual offences across the United States and following the helpline's success within the United States, the same approach has started to be adopted internationally. The UK Lucy Faithfull Foundation launched theirs in 2002, and the Netherlands followed suit in 2012. The Stop It Now! helpline is operated by trained staff who provide specialist advice and support; it is available as a call-in, call-back or online service. Where this intersects with the online world is associated with the Stop It Now! campaign. There has been an ongoing campaign across all forms of media to raise awareness of the helpline; this includes targeted, paid-for advertising across the clear and dark web. In addition to the use of the reThink chatbot for UK-based PornHub users, potential online offenders from other countries are directed to the Stop It Now! Helpline.

Education and collaboration

Internet Watch Foundation

In addition to some incredible technological solutions that have been developed and continue to be created by the IWF, they are continually researching and monitoring Internet trends. The IWF has been producing its annual report since 2005, which provides a comprehensive overview of the organisation's efforts to combat child sexual abuse online. It details the number of reports received, images and videos assessed and URLs taken down containing CSAM. The report also highlights emerging trends, such as the rise of "self-generated" material, where children are coerced or groomed into creating and sharing explicit content. The 2023 report highlighted some shocking statistics; in particular, there has been a 65% increase in self-generated CSAM among seven- to ten-year-olds since 2022. This is an increase of 1,816% since 2019 (Internet Watch Foundation, 2023).

The IWF's annual report offers valuable insights into the scale and nature of online child sexual abuse. It breaks down the data by age and gender of victims, type of content and geographical location of hosting. The report also includes case studies and testimonials, highlighting the impact of the IWF's work on survivors and their families. Additionally, it outlines the organisation's partnerships with law enforcement agencies, tech companies and non-governmental organisations (NGOs) in the fight against CSAM. For example, the IWF collaborated with the National Society for the Prevention of Cruelty to Children (NSPCC) to develop the 'Report-Remove' tool (NSPCC, n.d.) which allows young people to report an image or video shared online and to receive help in having it taken down. The child making the report is then supported by Childline throughout the process, such as being offered the counselling services and access to other online resources.

Understanding how people offend is critical to combat the rise in online offending; the IWF report is a globally recognised source of knowledge and serves to raise public awareness and educate stakeholders about the realities of online child sexual abuse. It sheds light on the problem's scale and the offenders' techniques. The data and insights presented in the annual report are crucial in informing policy discussions and advocacy efforts. By highlighting the latest trends and challenges, the report enables policymakers to develop robust legal frameworks and industry standards to combat online child sexual abuse. By identifying areas where further investigation is needed, the report encourages the development of advanced technology and tools for detecting and removing CSAM.

WeProtect global alliance

Another organisation that focuses on making the Internet a safer place for children through education, knowledge sharing and collaboration is the WeProtect Global Alliance. Founded in 2014 and launched as an independent organisation in 2020 through the merging of the European and U.S. Global Alliance Against Child Sexual Abuse Online and the UK-based WePROTECT, the WeProtect Global Alliance is a global effort to prevent child sexual abuse online. They have taken a unique approach by viewing the problem as similar to a long-term public health problem and spreading the message that this is a "public health emergency" (WeProtect Global Alliance, 2023). Their approach is one of collaboration, bringing together governments and private sector organisations to create a coordinated, multi-pronged approach to protecting children online.

The WeProtect Global Alliance collaborates with partners to conduct research and share knowledge. As part of this work, they produce a biennial Global Threat Assessment (GTA). This report details the risks and harms children face online and provides recommendations for change in key areas. These recommendations focus on critical areas such as technology, policy, society and criminal justice.

Education in schools

In discussing preventative strategies, we cannot ignore the importance of early education for children around the Internet. The Department for Education (DoE) published guidance on teaching online safety in schools in January 2023, highlighting the importance of teaching children about online safety in an age-appropriate way. The guidance is extensive and exhaustive about a range of relevant topics, including:

- How to evaluate what they see online
- How to recognise techniques for persuasion
- How and when to seek support
- How to stay safe online (including online abuse, radicalisation, challenges, fake profiles, content which incites, grooming, live streaming, pornography and unsafe comunication)
- How the Internet affects well-being

The DoE guidance also highlights the importance of schools reviewing, maintaining, embedding and modelling online safety principles. Additionally, an increasing number of online materials have been produced to assist professionals and parents in supporting children and young people in becoming more aware of online risks. One such example is the National Crime Agency's Child Exploitation and Online Protection (NCA-CEOP) Education team website, which includes helpful guidance for professionals, parents and children of different age groups. The NSPCC has also published various online resources, including a specific resource for children with Special Educational Needs and Disabilities (SEND), produced in collaboration with Ambitious about Autism. Additionally, Childnet has specific resources for children under five years old, recognising the increasing availability of devices for very young children (e.g. Ofcom, 2024).

The preceding chapters have focused on exploring the Internet, how people offend, how they get caught, and what preventative strategies exist. We will now consider how you can keep yourself safe online as a professional.

References

CEOP. (n.d.). Welcome to CEOP Education. Retrieved June 29, 2024, from https://www.ceopeducation.co.uk/

Childnet. (n.d.). 'Keeping under fives safe online'. Retrieved June 29, 2024, from https://www.childnet.com/help-and-advice/keeping-young-children-safe-online/

Department for Education. (2023). 'Guidance: Teaching online safety in schools'. Retrieved June 28, 2024, from https://www.gov.uk/government/publications/teaching-online-safety-in-schools/teaching-online-safety-in-schools

Internet Watch Foundation. (2023). *'Self-generated' Child Sex Abuse | IWF 2023 Annual Report*. Internet Watch Foundation. Retrieved June 28, 2024, from https://www.iwf.org.uk/annual-report-2023/trends-and-data/self-generated-child-sex-abuse/

Microsoft. (n.d.). *PhotoDNA*. Microsoft. Retrieved June 2, 2024, from https://www.microsoft.com/en-us/photodna

NSPCC. (n.d.). Online safety for families and children with SEND. Retrieved June 29, 2024 from https://www.nspcc.org.uk/keeping-children-safe/online-safety/online-safety-families-children-with-send/

NSPCC. (n.d.). Remove nude images shared online. Retrieved September 17, 2024, from https://www.nspcc.org.uk/keeping-children-safe/online-safety/online-reporting/report-remove/?gad_source=1&gclid=CjwKCAjw0aS3BhA3EiwAKaD2ZTA2JhQNCMcI08 BiV8Xb6FYaTGGoKSs8tIdxaq4r7sO4Rx7ezbl7MBoCA3sQAvD_BwE&gclsrc=aw.ds

Ofcom. (2024). Children and parents: Media use and attitudes report. Retrieved June 29, 2024 from chrome-extension://efaidnbmnnnibpcajpcglclefindmkaj/https://www.ofcom.org.uk/siteassets/resources/documents/research-and-data/media-literacy-research/children/children-media-use-and-attitudes-2024/childrens-media-literacy-report-2024.pdf

Scanlan, J., Prichard, J., Hall, L. C., Watters, P., & Wortley, R. (2024, March 5). *reThink chatbot evaluation*. University of Tasmania. Retrieved June 13, 2024, from https://figshare.utas.edu.au/articles/report/reThink_Chatbot_Evaluation/25320859

WeProtect Global Alliance. (2023). *Our strategy: 2023–2025*. WeProtect global alliance. Retrieved July 6, 2024, from https://www.weprotect.org/about-us/2023-2025-strategy/

9 How to keep yourself safe online

Christopher Wise

Introduction

Now that we have thoroughly examined online offending, it is time to discuss how to keep ourselves safe online as professionals. The following tips in the chapter are not exhaustive but are, as a security expert, my opinion of some of the most important ones. It is imperative to take precautions for those working with technologically savvy people who offend online, but this guidance applies to anyone who could be the target of cybercriminals, which in this day and age is almost anyone.

This chapter reviews the tools and practical steps you can apply daily to keep yourself safe when using the Internet. We will also consider the requirements of the Information Commissioner's Office (ICO) and the General Data Protection Regulation (GDPR) when handling personal information professionally. In particular, there has been a massive increase in cyberattacks against legal firms, with 65% of UK law firms reportedly being victims of cyberattacks (Murphy, 2023). Using these examples, we will highlight what protections could have prevented these attacks and how you can apply them.

Keeping data safe

When we talk about data, it is essential to consider that not all data is equal in its sensitivity, nor is it always obvious how sensitive a piece of data can be. For example, when we think about a work email address, we may not consider it particularly sensitive. However, unlike your personal email address, it is not only an email address but also includes where you work. For those familiar with working in secure environments, you have likely received training on data classifications.

For those unaware, data classifications are a way of marking a document's sensitivity and can typically be found in the footer of each page. Classifications provide a quick reference for anyone accessing a document, letting them know who they can share it with and how carefully it should be protected.

It may only be practical or relevant to some readers to go on and classify every document they have access to. However, thinking about these classifications when creating or accessing sensitive data can provide helpful context for how you should store and share that file. There are a variety of different ways of classifying data,

DOI: 10.4324/9781003543794-9

and many organisations have their internal definitions, but in general, data is classified as follows:

- Public – This is the least sensitive classification. Data in this category is not sensitive and is either already shared publicly or can be. This type of data includes promotional materials, publications and public-facing websites. No special considerations are required when handling this type of data.
- Internal – Data of this classification should only be viewed by an organisation's employees. Internal emails and communications that don't contain personal data or client data fall into this category. Data of this type should be handled carefully and not shared externally. There would be minimal impact if the data were exposed outside of an organisation.
- Confidential – This data is sensitive; it shouldn't be available to everyone, even within the same organisation. If the data is exposed publicly, it could damage an organisation's or your reputation, but there would be no legal or regulatory issue.
- Restricted – Restricted data is the most sensitive and includes personally identifiable information (PII), financial information and proprietary information. One or more regulatory frameworks could protect it, and if inadvertently shared, it could lead to fines or criminal charges. Specifically, this is the classification of data that GDPR and the ICO are concerned with.

GDPR requires that organisations classify data within a data inventory. The only distinction it makes is between non-personal and personal data. Personal data is then sub-categorised as either regular data (such as names and birth dates) or special category data (including financial, biometric, health data, both physical and mental, and sexual orientation). Special category data does not include criminal offence data as it has specific rules around its handling and processing. If you handle criminal offence data, I recommend reviewing GDPR guidance.

Now that we have a baseline understanding of what data should be considered sensitive and protected, we will examine how to protect that data.

Storing data securely

Exploring all of the methods used to store data securely is outside the scope of this chapter, but we will look at the approaches that should be taken when working with documents stored digitally on your devices.

The first thing to consider when working on a document is where you will save it. Are you using a cloud-based storage service like Google Drive or OneDrive or saving it locally to your laptop or PC? Certain services offer synchronisation capabilities, making the file available online and on your laptop, PC and mobile device. Ultimately, you are responsible for ensuring that a file is suitably protected "at rest", as we would say in the IT industry. However, you can be reasonably confident that cloud-based services will ensure your files are encrypted and only accessible to users with the correct permissions. That responsibility ends in the locations you control; this is where you need to ensure that your mobile phone, laptop, PC and any other devices have suitable protection.

The two key things to consider are encryption and access control. As we have covered in previous chapters, encryption is a complex mathematical process that makes data unreadable to anyone without a key. There are various "layers" that encryption can be applied to in the case of digital files; it is either the file itself that can be encrypted or the disk it is stored on. In highly secure environments, it can be both. It is generally considered that for most data, ensuring that the device it is stored upon is encrypted is sufficient. This means that even if your laptop is stolen, the thief cannot read the files from it. Almost all modern smartphones are encrypted by default; this is not true for laptops, desktops, PCs, USB drives or other external storage devices. If you need clarification on the encryption of any device you use for accessing and storing sensitive data, speak with an IT professional who can assist you in choosing and setting up suitably secured devices.

The second point, access control, is about ensuring that only approved people can access the data. You can have the best encryption in the world, but if your password is written on a Post-it note attached to your computer or set to something simple like "Password123!", it does not matter. I recommend following the National Cyber Security Centre password guidelines. The great news is that changing your password every 30 days is not recommended! Instead, use a different password for each application or service; use a password manager to generate random, complex passwords automatically and do not share your passwords with others. Where available, always use multi-factor authentication; this can be an application on your mobile phone or a specialised hardware key. Microsoft and Google provide an authenticator app that can be used across multiple platforms and services. Multi-factor authentication is critical when using an online storage provider like OneDrive or Google Drive.

Another area to consider when handling very sensitive data is any data sovereignty regulations that may apply. This is less of an issue for data you store on your computer or a USB drive, but when storing data in the cloud, you may need to investigate what options you have available for keeping the data within the UK, EU or US. Typically, this level of consideration is reserved for the most sensitive data, particularly healthcare-related data. Most well-known file storage providers offer the ability to specify what region your data is held in. If you are unsure of what regulatory frameworks the data you handle may be subject to, I recommend seeking some professional guidance on this and investigating what options you have available from your storage provider.

The ICO and GDPR require that data be stored safely and protected from unlawful processing or accidental loss, destruction or damage. However, they don't give specific or practical guidance on what that means. Ensuring that you have backups, use encryption, and limit access to only those who need it goes a long way towards meeting your obligations as a data owner.

One of the other core principles of GDPR covers data retention. This is how long you should retain personal data and a person's right to be forgotten. Data retention is complex and will vary based on the type of data content. GDPR does not dictate an appropriate amount of time, only that it is reviewed periodically and that data is only kept for as long as necessary. It is your job as a professional to understand the type of data you hold and, accordingly, the appropriate amount of time to retain it.

Sharing data safely

Now that we are confident that we are storing our most sensitive data securely, how do we share it with other people who need to access it safely? It may come as a surprise, but emailing a document is not considered exceptionally safe. This is because there are no guarantees of encryption; the servers that the email passes through on its way to the recipient could hold onto a copy of it for years, even decades, and you are one misspelling of an email address away from sharing it with the wrong person with no way to pull it back.

Some email-like systems are considered safe; these are built to be secure and only allow users to send emails to other users of the same secure system. One example system used within England and Wales is the Criminal Justice Secure Email (CJSM), which allows anyone working within the criminal justice system to exchange emails securely.

Only send sensitive information via email if you are sure you use a secure email service. If not, use a secure file storage service like Google Drive, OneDrive, DropBox or similar. These platforms allow you to grant and control access to files using a person's email address, but you can retain control of the file and even set the level of access a person has to a file; for example, you can make it read-only and prevent someone from downloading the file.

Working away from home

Public and untrusted WiFi networks

As we have covered in previous chapters, the rise of Hypertext Transfer Protocol Secure (HTTPS) and its use of encryption have generally made the Internet a much safer place. Any malicious person with access to a network will only be able to see what websites you are accessing, not the information being shared with it, and your passwords will remain safe, at least from snooping. However, that only makes public WiFi networks somewhat secure, and they are still a target for hackers and other technologically savvy individuals looking to steal people's credentials.

One of the more common attacks against WiFi networks is called an "evil twin" attack. This is a form of man-in-the-middle attack. To perform an evil twin attack, a threat actor uses specialised software to create their own WiFi network with the same name as the legitimate network. They can then send a signal that causes all devices connected to the good network to disconnect and reconnect. Any device closer to the perpetrator network will unwittingly join the evil network, acting as a man in the middle. Once the victims are connected to the evil network, the attacker can eavesdrop on communication or attempt to steal sensitive data, such as passwords or even credit card information.

If you must use a public or untrusted network, I recommend the following steps to protect yourself, and I have highlighted below some suspicious signs to look for:

- Use a VPN – Hopefully, your employer provides a corporate VPN solution. If not, I recommend investing in one for work and personal use.
- Tether to your phone as an alternative – "Tethering" is a feature supported by most smartphones that allows them to share their internet connection with your devices via Bluetooth or USB. This connection is dedicated to your devices, so using it is much safer than WiFi.
- Be wary of login pages– Most public WiFi networks use what are referred to as 'captive portals'. These pages are displayed when you connect, sometimes displaying terms and conditions, asking you to log in, or sometimes requesting payment for their use. Some attacks are available to cybercriminals that involve mimicking these pages to steal usernames, passwords or credit card information. I recommend setting up a dedicated or disposable email address and never entering payment information into any website unless you are entirely sure of its authenticity.
- One final point often overlooked is protecting what is visible on your screen. You never know who could be looking over your shoulder. Investing in a laptop privacy screen reduces the field of view of your laptop screen and makes it much harder for someone other than you to see what is on it.

Hacking/ransomware/phishing

Protecting yourself from these types of attacks can be challenging, especially when working in an organisation that sophisticated cybercriminals could target. Unfortunately, there is no one simple answer or tool you can install to prevent this type of attack entirely, but there are steps we can take:

- Be diligent. If you receive an unsolicited email, even from someone you know, check to ensure it is legitimate. Are there unusual file attachments or links? Is the request unusual? If it is an email from someone you know, contact them via a different means to check if they sent it.
- Only install software you're sure of. Most operating systems have checks that verify the validity of an application. If a warning is presented, be extremely careful when clicking OK. If in doubt, don't do it.
- Create regular backups and store them independently; this could be as simple as having a selection of encrypted portable storage drives used for different weeks or months. Some ransomware includes a delay, which gives cybercriminals a chance to corrupt or encrypt backups, and having multiple separate physical storage devices can help protect against this. Even if you lose some data, it is better than losing it all.

- Invest in anti-phishing software. There are some very effective commercial software providers for both businesses and consumers that provide some protection against phishing attacks.

Online presence

One of the methods hackers utilise is social engineering. This approach involves performing deep research into target businesses or individuals. They will use fake accounts and impersonate people you know or use the information to pass themselves off as a colleague or someone you know to trick the unsuspecting victim into giving up information or giving them access to a system. Social media platforms, including LinkedIn, are a valuable resource for gathering information about you; for those working in the criminal justice system, it is essential to keep publicly available information to a minimum.

One method is to use a pseudonym on your personal social media accounts to create a separation between your work and social profiles or simply not allow anyone to find your social profiles and only add people you know and trust. Similarly, keep your public information to a minimum for LinkedIn and be careful who you add to your network.

A particular area of concern is geotagging, which occurs when you take a photo using a mobile or modern digital camera, and the coordinates are embedded within the image. Even if you have disabled that option in your phone or camera, you can add the location when you upload the image to social media. This geographical information could be a risk when you take photos at home or in your local area, and it could lead to your address being inadvertently exposed online. Remember how much information a photo could provide about your location, and only share it with people you trust.

In Chapter 10, we will discuss the future of the Internet and how technology could advance in the next five to ten years.

References

Murphy, G. (2023, December 9). *65% of law firms have been a victim of a cyber incident.* The Law Society. Retrieved July 6, 2024, from https://www.lawsociety.org.uk/topics/blogs/are-you-the-65-percent-or-the-35-per-cent-65-percent-of-law-firms-cyber-attack-victim

10 The future of the Internet and offending considerations

Christopher Wise

Artificial intelligence and machine learning

As we have discussed in previous chapters, the recent explosion in the usage of artificial intelligence (AI) is having a significant impact on our society, and this is only the beginning. OpenAI's ChatGPT was initially released as a demo in November 2022. This first publicly accessible edition was GPT version 3, a purely conversational AI capable of impressive tasks. As of 2024, OpenAI has released GPT-4o; this version was able to pass the US legal bar exam but can also process and produce images, audio and video – it can even sing.

So, how does this advancement relate to the world of online offending? As we covered in Chapters 2 and 3, there are already "Dark AIs" available on the dark web for criminals to use. Unlike their monitored and secure cousins, they do not have any controls inhibiting the type of behaviours they will engage with. They are, however, limited in their capabilities, having only a fraction of the sophistication and accuracy of the first ChatGPT; this is very likely to change as the cost to develop and run more sophisticated AIs becomes lower than it is currently. Similar to language-based models that can create more convincing and sophisticated phishing campaigns, the availability and ease with which deepfake technology can perform vishing or more deepfake video-based scams will increase.

There have already been notable cases where millions of dollars have been scammed out of large organisations through the use of deepfake technology. This sophisticated type of attack is highly targeted and challenging to perform. In the future, the barrier to entry will inevitably decrease, and we will see an increasing number of deepfake scams. Through sophisticated automation and bots, these scams may impact your average internet user, not just large corporations.

To combat this inevitable trend, communication platforms must invest in technologies to help detect where deepfakes are being used. Thus, a new level of cat-and-mouse game will begin between online offenders, technology companies and law enforcement agencies protecting us from online crimes.

Virtual reality and the metaverse

The rise of virtual reality (VR) and the concept of the Metaverse – a persistent, shared virtual space where users interact with each other and digital objects

DOI: 10.4324/9781003543794-10

and environments – poses a challenge for law enforcement and policymakers. Within the UK, the first reported case of sexual harassment within the Metaverse was investigated by the police in January 2024 (Vallance, 2024). The incident was reported in late 2023, and the victim was under 16 at the time of the offence. She reported that she was "surrounded by three to four male-sounding and male-representing avatars, who started sexually harassing me in a verbal sense and then sexually assaulting my avatar". The sale of VR headsets declined in 2023 compared to previous years (Vanian, 2023). Still, despite this dip, analysts expect that while VR is struggling to break out of the niche gaming market, it will ultimately make it to the mainstream (International Data Corporation, 2024).

For as long as online virtual spaces have existed, there have been complaints of sexual harassment and abuse. The first reported case of virtual rape dates back to 1993 and took place in a text-only virtual environment LambdaMOO (MacKinnon, 1997). Debating the legal and moral points of whether the act of rape is possible within a virtual environment is out of the scope of this book. Still, one thing is for sure: as the usage of VR grows, the incidences of this type of behaviour will likely increase, and the creators of these spaces and law makers will need to consider the impact these behaviours can have on their victims.

Another concern is the possibility of theft and fraud within the virtual economies within the Metaverse. Virtual economies already exist and have real-world values associated with them. To give an example of the value some digital assets can carry, metaverse companies have started to sell virtual real estate, the most expensive of which sold for five million USD in 2022 (Curzio Research, 2022). Whilst the theft of virtual real estate is unlikely, other digital assets will inevitably become the target of hackers or other virtual scams.

Quantum computing

One of the most exciting recent developments in the world of computers is quantum computing. In traditional computing, everything is processed using bits; a bit is represented by a 0 or 1, on or off. Quantum computers use qubits that can be 0, 1 or both. This is because they use the principles of quantum mechanics, where particles can exist in multiple states at once. If we use the example of a computer trying to find its way out of a maze, a traditional computer would try each path, one after the other, until it found its way out. A quantum computer can try every path at the same time.

Quantum computers are specialised, and it is unlikely that every home will have one. However, they promise considerable advancements in discovering new medicines and materials, AI and machine learning, and climate modelling.

So, how does quantum computing represent a future cyber threat? The answer is in its ability to try every path in a maze simultaneously and what this means for encryption. In Chapter 4, we discussed how encryption works and how long it would take for current computers to crack an encryption algorithm. Modern encryption algorithms could take decades and vast amounts of computing power;

due to a quantum computer's ability to try all possible combinations simultaneously, decades could become minutes. The threat quantum computers represent is already changing how we approach encryption. Organisations have started to develop post-quantum cryptography, and businesses are urged to move to these improved encryption standards (H, 2023).

Quantum computing is still in its infancy, and analysts believe we may not have a fully capable quantum computer by 2040 (Gao et al., 2023). One thing that is certain is that when we do, all technology companies need to be prepared for the shift required in encryption to keep our data safe.

Internet of Things

The number of internet-connected devices in our homes has exploded in the last few years. As of 2024, the average number of devices per home is 18. This number is expected to increase to 32.1 by 2030 (Vailshery, 2024). Within cybersecurity, we talk a lot about attack surfaces. This measures and describes all the weak spots and vulnerabilities a malicious party could use to gain access to or attack our systems. As the size of an organisation increases, so does the number of devices and applications in use, and thus, the greater its attack surface.

As our homes become more connected, so does our personal attack surface. There have already been reported cases of smart devices being compromised by hackers. As early as 2014, it was discovered that a cyberattack was using hacked smart home appliances to send spam emails (NBC News, 2014).

We may think hacking our smart home devices does not cause much harm. However, the amount of data hackers can collect and the ability for hackers to move between devices once they have found a virtual door into your home should not be underestimated. In addition, many smart home devices include cameras, and even smart fridge freezers can include a camera and a microphone.

This risk extends beyond the home and into industry as well. The 2007 Stuxnet computer virus is a warning that digital threats can have consequences in the real world. Even today, precisely who is responsible for releasing this virus to the world has never been confirmed. Although the evidence suggests a collaboration between Israel and the US, this was the first time a computer virus damaged industrial equipment. The Iranian government never officially confirmed it; however, this virus was designed to seek out industrial control software and monitor it. When it had enough information, it triggered a centrifuge to spin so fast it destroyed itself. On that occasion, the virus attacked an Iranian uranium enrichment plant.

As the number of Internet of Things (IoT) devices increases, state-sponsored cyberattacks will likely increase. Manufacturers and governments must consider the implications for critical national infrastructure and secure it accordingly.

Distributed web

So, what is next for the Internet itself? Fundamentally, the Internet has mostly stayed the same since its inception over 40 years ago. It has grown and advanced, but the heart of it is very much the same. The next internet iteration is described as the distributed web or Web3. There is no single inventor or creator for this change in the Internet; it is an evolution of the existing Internet into something decentralised where its users control their data, and security and privacy are built into its foundations.

In 2009, 20 years after Tim Berners-Lee invented the Internet, he began documenting design issues he saw (Berners-Lee, 2009). Fundamentally, he saw that the Internet had moved from being decentralised, where anyone could publish and host a website, to being controlled by a small number of massive tech companies. In particular, social media platforms own and control their users' data. Berners-Lee proposed a new "socially aware cloud storage" (Berners-Lee, 2009). He believed that the Web had failed to serve humanity and that the increasing centralisation had created an "anti-human" phenomenon (Brooker, 2018).

To solve this problem, Tim Berners-Lee has started an open-source project known as Solid (Social Linked Data) to decentralise the Internet, starting with our data. This project aims to put users in control of their data and take it out of the hands of big tech. This approach is just one of the technologies and changes underpinning the future distributed Internet.

Blockchain, which supports cryptocurrencies, and peer-to-peer (P2P) networks are two other cornerstone technologies that will facilitate the distributed Web. A P2P network is a decentralised communication model where each participating computer or device, known as a peer, has equal capabilities and responsibilities. Unlike traditional client-server models, where a central server manages and distributes resources, such as the websites we access today, P2P networks distribute tasks and workloads among peers. When accessing a website or downloading a file from a P2P network, the security built into these networks means you do not know who owns or created the content.

The absence of a central authority and the potential for enhanced anonymity that these technologies create will make policing the distributed web challenging for law enforcement. On the positive side, the era of our data being stolen and sold on the dark web to the highest bidder and controlled by large corporations should end.

It is uncertain how long it will be before your typical internet user becomes aware of the distributed web, and it becomes a part of our daily lives; the convenience of a centralised web and our acceptance of it makes it difficult to predict when we will see this shift, but much like a snowball rolling down a mountain, we will reach a critical mass where even big tech will have to change their approach to support this growing movement of a person's right to own and control their data.

Concluding thoughts

As we have explored, the digital landscape is complex and ever evolving. With its vast potential for connection and innovation, the Internet has become fertile ground for criminal activity which will only continue to evolve in sophistication. It is the role of professionals in the criminal justice system to stay ahead of those evolutions if we are to successfully understand and tackle online offending.

In the next concluding chapter, we will draw together some of the key messages from this book, consider the impact of online sexual offending in particular, and discuss ways that we can, as professionals, keep our knowledge current.

References

Berners-Lee, T. (2009, August 16). *Read-write linked data.* World Wide Web Consortium. https://www.w3.org/DesignIssues/ReadWriteLinkedData.html

Berners-Lee, T. (2009, August 17). *Socially aware cloud storage - Design Issues.* W3C. Retrieved August 2, 2024, from https://www.w3.org/DesignIssues/CloudStorage.html

Brooker, K. (2018, July 1). *"I Was Devastated": The man who created the World Wide Web has some regrets.* Vanity Fair. https://www.vanityfair.com/news/2018/07/the-man-who-created-the-world-wide-web-has-some-regrets

Curzio Research. (2022, May 24). Largest land deal in metaverse history just announced. PR Newswire. Retrieved July 28, 2024, from https://www.prnewswire.com/news-releases/largest-land-deal-in-metaverse-history-just-announced-301554502.html

Gao, S., Gschwendtner, M., Hijazi, H., Morgan, N., & Soller, H. (2023, May 19). *Is winter coming? Quantum computing's trajectory in the years ahead.* McKinsey. Retrieved July 28, 2024, from https://www.mckinsey.com/capabilities/mckinsey-digital/our-insights/tech-forward/is-winter-coming-quantum-computings-trajectory-in-the-years-ahead

H, J. (2023, November 3). *Migrating to post-quantum cryptography - NCSC.GOV.UK.* National Cyber Security Centre. Retrieved July 28, 2024, from https://www.ncsc.gov.uk/blog-post/migrating-to-post-quantum-cryptography-pqc

International Data Corporation (IDC). (2024, March 19). *IDC forecasts Robust growth for AR/VR headset shipments fueled by the rise of mixed reality.* IDC. Retrieved July 27, 2024, from https://www.idc.com/getdoc.jsp?containerId=prUS51971224

MacKinnon, R. (1997, March 1). Virtual rape. *Journal of Computer-Mediated Communication, 2*(4). https://academic.oup.com/jcmc/article/2/4/JCMC247/4584404

NBC News. (2014, January 18). *Smart refrigerators hacked to send out spam: Report.* NBCNews.https://www.nbcnews.com/tech/internet/smart-refrigerators-hacked-send-out-spam-report-n11946

Vailshery, L. S. (2024, June 12). *IoT connections worldwide 2022–2033.* Statista. Retrieved July 28, 2024, from https://www.statista.com/statistics/1183457/iot-connected-devices-worldwide/

Vallance, C. (2024, January 2). *Police investigate virtual sex assault on girl's avatar.* BBC. https://www.bbc.co.uk/news/technology-67865327

Vanian, J. (2023, December 19). *VR market shrinking as meta pours billions of dollars into metaverse.* CNBC. https://www.cnbc.com/2023/12/19/vr-market-shrinking-as-meta-pours-billions-of-dollars-into-metaverse.html

Concluding thoughts

Jennifer Bamford

The victims[1] of online sexual offending

Ultimately, what we have tried to do within this book is to educate and therefore empower those who are working hard to apprehend, understand, assess and treat those who have committed online offences in order to reduce offending (and reoffending) and to prevent further victims. However, the scale of the impact of all forms of online offending cannot be ignored. This is especially the case, we would argue, for those who have been the victims of online sexual offending, and this chapter will reflect on the groups of individuals potentially impacted by this endemic form of crime.

Victims in the images

The most obvious victim group of online sexual offenders are the individuals who are targeted: the children who are abused within the images which are then shared online; the children who are groomed, coerced, bullied or threatened into sending images or meeting with an offender; the women whose sexual images are shared online without their consent; the people who are trafficked aided by online communication; and so on.

The consequences for victims of sexual abuse can span decades and affect broad areas of their future life, including difficulties within intimate relationships (Colman & Widom, 2004), self-destructive behaviours (Fergusson et al., 2008), substance misuse (Kendler et al., 2000), sexual difficulties (Noll et al., 2003) and re-victimisation (Noll et al., 2003).

Elly Hanson (2017) explored a range of factors that might impact the degree of victim harm, including social contextual factors such as familial support; research has found that parental reactions to disclosure of online grooming can be diverse (Quayle et al., 2012) and sometimes harsh and punitive (Whittle et al., 2013), which can further traumatise a child who has disclosed abuse. For children who have produced self-generated imagery, often as a consequence of being coerced or threatened, there may be complicated negative emotions attached to their behaviour, including shame and self-blame (Jonsson & Svedin, 2012). As some abusive imagery is made to look as though the victim is accepting or enjoying the

DOI: 10.4324/9781003543794-11

abuse, this fear of being viewed as complicit or responsible can prevent disclosure in victims (Palmer & Stacey, 2004). This lack of early disclosure then leaves a victim open to repeat abuse, compounding their psychological distress. However, the idea of disclosure and the likely possibility that their image might then be seen by law enforcement and possibly their own families can feel intolerable.

For those whose abusive images are shared online, there is the element of permanence and a lack of control that exacerbates harm. They can feel fearful and paranoid about seeing their abusive images online (e.g. see Sharon Cooper's 2012 written testimony before the US Sentencing Commission), and this brings a sense of helplessness that often prolongs their own recovery. That mental state can, and sadly has, led to young people taking their own lives. Victims also sometimes report feeling mistreated by the legal system, which can compound the impact of the abuse (Kunst et al., 2015). As adversarial as the legal system is, it remains essential that victims of online sexual offending are treated compassionately and sensitively, and that families are given the proper support in caring for their loved one.

The offenders' family as victims

The family members of a perpetrator of online sexual offending are an often overlooked group of victims. After a loved one has been apprehended, the partner and/ or children are left in a difficult position, practically and emotionally. They are often left feeling conflicting emotions of betrayal, anger and loss whilst also dealing with the reality of a reduced income, the loss of a parent and the possible breakdown of a relationship.

In a scenario where the perpetrator has a child, the non-offending partner will often be required to engage with an assessment by Children's Services, which can feel intrusive and challenging. They may be assessed as to their suitability to care for the child as a sole parent and be judged as to their protective capacity, a situation and set of circumstances they may never have considered or predicted, which can feel overwhelming. Research suggests that partners of sexual offenders can be subject to 'courtesy stigma' (Farkas & Miller, 2007) and often feel judged and misunderstood by professionals (Calhane et al., 2013). Additionally, it may be very difficult for others to understand why a non-offending partner may wish to support their partner, and they may experience rejection and abandonment from others in their social circle as a result of this (Duncan et al., 2020).

Encouragingly, there has been increasing awareness of the need to support non-offending partners. Organisations such as The Lucy Faithfull Foundation offer a programme called 'Inform' specifically for family/friends of online sexual offenders to support them and to help them understand the behavioural processes involved in online sexual offending. Additionally, Lincolnshire Police's POLIT (Police OnLine Investigation Unit) have introduced the role of an Indirect Victim Support Officer whose job it is to support the partners and children of someone under investigation for online sexual offending. It is hoped that similar initiatives might be introduced across other areas of the UK.

The online sexual offender as a victim

It may feel uncomfortable to consider the person who has offended as a victim, which is an understandable response given that they have been the source of harm. However, if we are to reduce re-offending and treat someone's problematic behaviour, we must have the capacity to compassionately understand them and what has led them to the point of causing harm. Research into those who engage in sexually harmful behaviour has consistently revealed a higher proportion of Adverse Childhood Experiences (ACEs) than those without a history of offending (Levenson et al., 2016). Specifically, sexual abuse is a risk factor commonly seen in populations of those who engage in sexually harmful behaviour (Jespersen et al., 2009). This is important when considering an individual's risk factors and treatment needs.

In Chapter 1, we talk about the role that legal online pornography plays and for some of our clients, this habitual use becomes compulsive, addictive and highly damaging. A 2014 study completed by Voon et al. found that neural differences in the processing of sexual-cue reactivity were identified in regions of the brain previously implicated in drug-cue reactivity studies, highlighting the potentially powerful and addictive nature of pornographic images. With increasing exposure, the individual can become desensitised and requires a higher intensity to maintain the same reward; this is where we often see clients who have started to become reckless in their online searches.

We raise these studies as examples of the various risk factors that might have played a role in someone's pathway to offending whilst acknowledging that, ultimately, those with capacity have responsibility for their behaviour and they have made the choice to do harm.

The professionals involved

In the life cycle of catching a perpetrator, the police are often the first to come into contact with Child Sexual Abuse Material (CSAM); this may be a police investigator or a forensic examiner, for example. The images can, understandably, be incredibly disturbing. Research has demonstrated that investigators of CSAM are vulnerable to experiencing a range of difficulties as a consequence of their exposure, including problems with post-traumatic stress symptoms, isolation from colleagues, overprotectiveness of family members, heightened awareness of child exploitation and mental health difficulties such as mood swings, exhaustion, sleep deprivation and numbness (Burns et al., 2008).

Other professionals working with sexual offenders can also experience negative side effects. It is well established in research that therapists who work with sex offenders can be impacted by their work, including the burden of accountability (Edmunds, 1997) and vicarious trauma (Moulden & Firestone, 2007). Gender-focused research by Baum & Moyal (2018) has concluded that male and female therapists demonstrate similar levels of burnout and disruption of sexual life, although male therapists experience significantly higher levels of vicarious trauma.

The apprehension and rehabilitation of people who commit sexual offences online is important work, but it would be remiss not to acknowledge the human vulnerability of professionals involved in this process.

Where do we go from here?

Throughout this book, we have navigated the intricacies of the Internet, delving into its underlying technologies, the various forms of cybercrime that exploit them and the organisations tirelessly working to combat these threats. As a professional working in the criminal justice system (e.g. psychologists, social workers, probation officers, solicitors, etc), you do not need to be a technical expert, but understanding some of the key principles of how people offend online will make you a more effective expert in your field.

We hope that this knowledge will help you to challenge clients more effectively, signpost them to the right agencies, treat them appropriately, manage their risk in an informed way and represent them better. This book is not exhaustive, but we hope it has given you a foundational understanding and a starting point for further learning. Indeed, as technology advances at an unprecedented pace, so will the methods and motivations of those who have offended online. The challenge for those working in the criminal justice system is to remain adaptable and informed, continually updating their knowledge base to address the ever-changing landscape of online offending effectively.

You might be questioning the relevance of this book in five, ten or 20 years' time, and this is a valid consideration given the rapidity of technological advancements. For this reason, we will be publishing relevant updates and providing online training events at the website: cyberwise.courses, where we take a deep dive into some of the topics covered in this book, as well as further topics related to the Internet and online offending.

Note

1 We have used the word 'victim' in this chapter as the focus is on those who have suffered significant negative consequences as a result of online offending. We do appreciate that many victims prefer to refer to themselves as survivors and some individuals who have experienced abuse do go on to show post-traumatic growth and recovery.

References

Baum, N., & Moyal, S. (2018). Impact on therapists working with sex offenders: A systematic review of gender finding. *Trauma, Violence & Abuse, 21*(1), 193–205.

Burns, C. M., Morley, J., Bradshaw, R., & Domene, J. (2008). The emotional impact on and coping strategies employed by police teams investigating internet child exploitation. *Traumatology, 14*(2), 20–31.

Calhane, H., Parker, G., & Duff, S. (2013). Treatment implications arising from a qualitative analysis of letters written by the nonoffending partners of men who have perpetrated child sexual abuse. *Journal of Child Sexual Abuse, 22*(6), 720–741.

Colman, R. A., & Widom, C. S. (2004). Childhood abuse and neglect and adult intimate relationships: A prospective study. *Child Abuse and Neglect, 28*, 1133–1151.

Cooper, S. W. (2012). The impact on children who have been victims of child pornography. Written testimony before the U.S. Sentencing Commission.

Duncan, K., Wakeham, A., Winder, B., Armitage, R., Roberts, L., & Blagden, N. (2020). *The experiences of non-offending partners of individuals who have committed sexual offences: Recommendations for practitioners and stakeholders.* https://huddersfield.box.com/s/1sumdnyq9yjkgwhw0axzvgt7e2rfgcih

Edmunds, S. B. (1997). The personal impact of working with sex offenders. In S. B. Edmunds (Ed.), *Impact: Working with sexual abusers* (p. 1130). Brandon, VT: Safer Society Press.

Farkas, M. A., & Miller, G. (2007). Reentry and reintegration: Challenges faced by the families of convicted sex offenders. *Federal Sentencing Reporter, 20*(1), 88–92.

Fergusson, D. M., Boden, J. M., & Horwood, L. J. (2008). Exposure to childhood sexual and physical abuse and adjustment in early adulthood. *Child Abuse and Neglect, 32*, 607–619.

Hanson, E. (2017). The impact of online sexual abuse on children and young people. In J. Brown (Ed.), *Online risk to children: Impact, protection and prevention* (pp. 97–122). Wiley Blackwell. https://doi.org/10.1002/9781118977545.ch6

Hamilton-Giachritsis, C., Hanson, E., Whittle, H. C., & Beech, A. R. (2017). *"Everyone deserves to be happy and safe" A mixed methods study exploring how online and offline child sexual abuse impact young people and how professionals respond to it.* London: NSPCC.

Jespersen, A. F., Lalumière, M. L., & Seto, M. C. (2009). Sexual abuse history among adult sex offenders and non sex offenders: A meta analysis. *Child Abuse and Neglect, 33*(3), 179–192.

Jonsson, L., & Svedin, C. G. (2012). Children within the images. In E. Quayle & K. M. Ribisl (Eds.), *Understanding and preventing online sexual exploitation of children* (pp. 23–43). Abingdon, OX, UK: Routledge.

Kendler, K. S., Bulik, C. M., Silberg, J., Hettema, J. M., Myers, J., & Prescott, C. A. (2000). Childhood sexual abuse and adult psychiatric and substance use disorders in women: An epidemiological and co-twin control analysis. *Archives of General Psychiatry, 57*, 953–959.

Kunst, M., Popelier, L., & Varekamp, E. (2015). Victim satisfaction with the criminal justice system and emotional recovery: A systematic and critical review of the literature. *Trauma, Violence, & Abuse, 16*(3), 336–358.

Levenson, J. S., Willis, G. M., & Prescott, D. S. (2016). Adverse childhood experiences in the lives of male sex offenders: Implications for trauma-informed care. *Sex Abuse, 28*(4), 340–359.

Moulden, H. M., & Firestone, P. (2007). Vicarious traumatization: The impact on therapists who work with sexual offenders. *Trauma, Violence & Abuse, 8*(1), 67–83.

Noll, J. G., Horowitz, L. A., Bonanno, G. A., Trickett, P. K., & Putnam, F. W. (2003). Revictimization and self-harm in females who experienced childhood sexual abuse: Results from a prospective study. *Journal of Interpersonal Violence, 18*, 1452–1471.

Noll, J. G., Trickett, P. K., & Putnam, F. W. (2003). A prospective investigation of the impact of childhood sexual abuse on the development of sexuality. *Journal of Consulting and Clinical Psychology, 71*, 575–586.

Palmer, T., & Stacey, L. (2004). *Just one click: Sexual abuse of children and young people through the internet and mobile phone technology.* Barkingside: Barnardo's.

Quayle, E., Jonsson, L., & Loof, L. (2012). *Online behaviour related to child sexual abuse: Interviews with affected young people.* Stockholm, Sweden: Council of the Baltic Sea States, ROBERT Project.

Voon, V., Mole, T. B., Banca, P., Porter, L., Morris, L., Mitchell, S., Lapa, T. R., Karr, J., Harrison, N. A., Potenza, M. N., & Irvine, M. (2014). Neural correlates of sexual cue reactivity in individuals with and without compulsive sexual behaviours. *PLoS One, 9*(7), Article e102419.

Whittle, H. C., Hamilton-Giachritsis, C. E., & Beech, A. R. (2013). Victim's voices: The impact of online grooming and sexual abuse. *Universal Journal of Psychology, 1*, 59–71.

Index

Note: Page numbers followed by "n" denote endnotes.

Printed in the United States
by Baker & Taylor Publisher Services